Candy Making
Basics

Evelyn Howe Fryatt

Sterling Publishing Co., Inc.
New York
A STERLING/TAMOS BOOK

A Sterling/Tamos Book

Originally published in hard cover as
Candy Making for Beginners
© 1996 by Evelyn Howe Fryatt

10   9   8   7   6   5

First paperback edition published in 1999 by
Sterling Publishing Co., Inc.
387 Park Avenue South, New York, NY 10016

TAMOS Books Inc.
300 Wales Avenue, Winnipeg, MB, Canada R2M
2S9

Distributed in Canada by Sterling Publishing
c/o Canadian Manda Group, One Atlantic Avenue,
Suite 105
Toronto, Ontario, Canada M6K 3E7
Distributed in Great Britain and Europe by
Chris Lloyd at Orca Book Services,
Stanley House, Fleets Lane,
Poole BH15 3AJ England
Distributed in Australia by Capricorn Link
(Australia) Pty Ltd.
P.O. Box 704, Windsor, NSW 2756 Australia

Design: Arlene Osen
Photography: Jerry Grajewski, Custom Images Ltd.
Printed in China

Canadian Cataloging-in-Publication Data
Fryatt, Evelyn Howe 1939–
    Candy making for beginners
    "A Sterling/Tamos book."
    Includes index.
    ISBN 1-895569-03-6
1. Candy. I. Title.
TX791.F79 1996   641.8'53   C96-920008-0

Library of Congress Cataloging-in-Publication Data
Fryatt, Evelyn Howe 1939–
    Candy making for beginners / Evelyn Howe
Fryatt.
        p.   cm.
    "A Sterling/Tamos book."
    Includes index.
    ISBN 1-895569-03-6
    1. Candy. I. Title.
TX791.F916 1996   96-11996
641.8'53--dc20   CIP

ISBN 1-895569-03-6 Trade
     1-895569-25-7 Paper

Contents

Recipes

Fudge Delights

Creamy Caramels

Easy Fondants

Terrific Truffles

Scrumptious Toffee

Party Morsels

Holiday Surprises

Kids Can Do It

—Tips from Evelyn—

I love sweets so I like to have some homemade candy on hand to enjoy now and then. And when I put in my own wholesome ingredients and flavorings I know that the candy I make will be just the way I like it. Of course I want to be sure that what I make is always successful. Over the years I've developed some tried-and-true methods for cooked candies that give me perfect results every time. My secrets are basic but very important. How do they work? Let me share these tips with you. I know you'll find them helpful.

Always read the recipe before you start to cook. Be sure you have the ingredients you need.

Always use a candy thermometer. They aren't expensive and using this little tool to judge how long to cook the candy mixture is so critical for toffees, fondants, and fudge. Be sure to immerse the entire bulb in the boiling syrup, do not rest it on the bottom of the pan, and always read it at eye level.

Double check the candy temperature using the cold water method. I use this method first when the candy thermometer *nears* the required temperature. Often the candy is ready *before* the temperature suggested in the recipe. Using both methods takes the guessing out of candy making.

Use a deep, heavy saucepan. Syrups rise as they boil so you'll need a pan with four times the capacity of the ingredients you use to prevent overflow. Choose cast iron, heavy aluminum, or stainless steel to allow syrups to cook evenly without burning. Scorched candy has to be thrown out.

Stir with a long-handled wooden spoon. Wood does not conduct heat so temperature of syrup will be more accurate. The long handle will also keep your hand away from splashes from the hot liquid.

When you put candy on to cook, stir the sugar until it is completely dissolved and comes to a boil, then stir only enough to prevent sticking to the pan and scorching.

As candy cooks, remove any sugar crystals on the side of the pan with a pastry brush dipped in hot water. This prevents large crystals from forming and keeps candy from being grainy. This is important for fudge, caramels, toffee, and hard crack candy.

Cool candy to lukewarm at room temperature before beating, unless otherwise instructed. (Do not cool in the refrigerator or freezer.) Use a heavy duty electric mixer or wooden spoon and beat cooled candy until it starts to firm. Pour into pan immediately.

These tips are really simple, but if you follow them I'm sure they will make a difference in the outcome of your candy making.

E. H. F.

Candy Making Basics

EQUIPMENT

Most items needed for successful candy making are already in your kitchen. If you need a few special pieces you will find them in the housewares section of department stores and candy supply shops.

Saucepans should be heavy gauge cast iron, copper, aluminum, or stainless steel with a flat bottom. Candy syrups heat unevenly and burn in thin saucepans. Choose a pan that has four times the capacity of the ingredients so boiling liquid will not overflow. Recipes containing milk increase by three times during cooking. Watch boiling mixtures carefully.

Pans for cooling candy can be cake pans (square or oblong). Choose 8- or 9-inch square pans, 13 x 9 x 2 inch oblong, 15-1/2 x 10-1/2 x 1 inch jelly roll pan, 9 x 5 x 3 inch or 8 x 4 x 2-1/2 inch loaf pans, or flat cookie sheets.

Pans for molding candy are available in metal or plastic for hard candies and chocolate. Special lollipop molds allow the stick to be put in place before pouring the candy.

Candy cups for chocolate or candies are small paper or foil containers. They are available in a variety of colors.

Wrapping foil, cellophane, or plastic for individual candies can be heavy or transparent. Foil, cellophane, and plastic wrap are available in a variety of colors.

Beater A heavy-duty electric mixer is recommended for beating fudge and other candy. A strong wooden spoon can also be used.

Metal palette knives are strong and flexible and useful for spreading candies and turning toffee.

Scissors are needed for cutting toffees and pull candies.

Mixing bowls can be small, medium, or large, made from plastic, metal, or glass. Choose microwave-safe bowls and cups to use in the microwave.

Measuring cups and spoons can be metal or plastic for measuring dry and liquid ingredients.

Oven mitts for handling hot pans.

Dipping spoons are useful when dipping candy in melted flavored candy coatings or caramel.

Wire cooling racks, pastry brush, airtight containers for storing candies, sucker sticks

INGREDIENTS

Candy is wonderfully rich and sweet—a delicious treat made from a variety of ingredients from your own kitchen.

Sugars suitable for the kind of candy you are making are indicated in the recipes. Granulated white sugar dissolves easily and is used most often. Brown sugar (light or dark) adds a caramel flavor and powdered sugar gives a smooth texture to uncooked candies. Corn syrup is a liquid sweetener used in candy making to prevent graininess (sugar crystal formation). But when too much is used the candy becomes soft and sticky. Molasses and honey add sweetness plus their own distinctive flavor.

NOTE *Powdered sugar has cornstarch added. It can also be called icing sugar.* When making uncooked candy it is especially important to use sugar with cornstarch added which acts as a thickener. *Check the ingredients on the package* to be sure you have the kind of sugar you need for the recipe.

Milk & cream are used in these recipes. Whole milk gives candy a rich flavor. Half and half and whipping cream add richness and flavor. Low-fat milk can be used to replace milk but the candy will be less rich. Evaporated milk is whole milk with 60 percent of the water removed. Low-fat dry milk has fat and water removed to make a powder. It gives flavor and texture to uncooked candies. Sweetened condensed milk is whole milk that has 50 percent of the water removed and sugar added. It adds flavor and sweetness to cooked and uncooked candies. I've included an economical way to make your own sweetened condensed milk (p15).

Chocolate comes in many forms. Unsweetened chocolate comes in squares and is used for cooking. It is pure hardened chocolate liquor. Semi-sweet chocolate is unsweetened chocolate with sugar, extra cocoa butter, and flavorings added. This chocolate is molded into squares or chips and used mainly for cooking. Milk chocolate is pure hardened chocolate liquor with more sugar, cocoa butter, flavoring, and milk solids added. It is good to eat and comes in squares, bars, and chips. Cocoa is chocolate with most of the cocoa butter removed from the chocolate liquor. The solid that's left is ground into a fine powder. No sugar or flavoring is added. Cocoa contains the least fat of any chocolate. Chocolate syrup is also low in fat. It is a combination of cocoa, corn syrup, and flavoring.

White chocolate is not real chocolate because it has no chocolate liquor but it does have cocoa butter.

Chocolate-flavored candy coatings use vegetable fat instead of cocoa butter and have coloring and flavoring added. They are not real chocolate (contains no chocolate liquor or cocoa butter).

Candy coatings come in white and pastel colors and have a vanilla flavor, or light and dark brown colors and have a milk or semi-sweet chocolate flavor. Candy coatings are sold in wafers. They are easier to use than real chocolate and work very well for molding and dipping. Pastel candy coatings can be flavored using oil flavoring.

Recipes in this book use melted chocolate and coatings to cover chocolates. Tempered chocolate, which is more difficult to prepare, is not used here.

HOW LONG TO COOK CANDY

Using a candy thermometer

Immerse bulb of thermometer in boiling mixture. Cook until desired temperature is reached.

Check your candy thermometer for accuracy

Place bulb of thermometer in a pan of rapidly boiling water. Read temperature without removing thermometer. It should read 212°F or 100°C.

NOTE Both humidity and altitude affect candy making. On humid days cook candy 1 degree higher than the recipe states. But if you live in the mountains cook the candy 1 to 2 degrees lower, since liquid boils at a lower temperature at higher altitudes.

Using a cold water method

Put a small amount of the hot mixture into a cup of cold (*not ice*) water. Remove the cooled mixture with your fingers. Test for the desired ball or thread stage, as shown. Continue cooking until desired stage is reached.

SOFT BALL STAGE (234° to 240°F)—Use for fudge, penuche, and fondants. Mixture can be rolled into a soft ball that does not hold its shape when removed from water.

SOFT BALL STAGE

FIRM BALL STAGE (244° to 248°F)—Use for soft caramels (fillings and turtles) and caramel corn. Mixture can be rolled into a firm ball that holds its shape softly when removed from water.

HARD BALL STAGE (250° to 260°F)—Use for divinity, toffee, nougats, and marshmallows. Mixture can be rolled into a firm ball.

SOFT CRACK STAGE (270° to 284°F)—Use for toffee and butterscotch. Mixture can be stretched into threads that are hard but elastic.

HARD CRACK STAGE (300° to 308°F)—Use for brittles, candy apples, and caramel candies. Mixture can be stretched into hard, brittle threads.

FIRM BALL STAGE

HARD BALL STAGE

SOFT CRACK STAGE

HARD CRACK STAGE

HOW TO MELT CHOCOLATE
Double Boiler Method
Chop up chocolate squares (chips and coatings do not need to be chopped) and put chocolate in the top of a dry double boiler. Put hot tap water in the bottom pan of the double boiler. Do not put on stove. Replace hot tap water if needed. Do not cover chocolate. Stir occasionally until melted. Use this method for melting coatings.

If you need only a small amount of colored coatings try melting them in an electric fry pan. Place the various colors each in separate clean wide-mouthed glass jars and set in frying pan. Set dial on WARM and stir until melted.

Microwave Method
Place chocolate in a microwave-safe bowl or glass measuring cup. Microwave until melted, according to chart, stirring two or three times.

NOTE Some microwave ovens are faster than others so coatings will melt in a shorter time. Check when you stir. Microwave *only until melted.*

Kind of chocolate	Amount	Minutes—*power* MEDIUM
CHIPS	1/2 to 1 cup	2 to 3
	1-1/2 cups	3 to 3-1/2
	2 cups	3-1/2 to 4
SQUARES	1 to 2 squares	1-1/2 to 2
	3 squares	2
	4 to 5 squares	2 to 2-1/2
	6 squares	2-1/2 to 3
COATINGS	2 to 3 cups	5—*power* DEFROST

HOW TO DIP CHOCOLATES
It takes approximately 1 pound of coatings to cover 1 pound of centers (40 to 50 pieces). Melt coatings using the double boiler method above. Using a dipping spoon, dip centers in melted coatings. Place on wax paper to set.

NOTE Keep coatings stirred when dipping. If coatings cool and thicken, add warm water to the bottom of the double boiler. The temperature of the room is also important when dipping centers. Keep room between 60° and 70°F. Store dipped centers at room temperature or in a cool place.

HOW TO SUBSTITUTE FOR CHOCOLATE IF YOU WANT LESS FAT

Instead of this	Try this
1-ounce square unsweetened chocolate	3 tablespoons cocoa powder plus 1 tablespoon vegetable shortening
1 ounce semi-sweet chocolate	3 tablespoons semi-sweet chocolate chips
1 cup semi-sweet chocolate chips	6 tablepsoons cocoa powder, 1/3 cup sugar plus 1/4 cup vegetable shortening
4-ounce bar sweet baking chocolate	1/4 cup cocoa powder, 1/3 cup sugar, plus 3 tablespoons vegetable shortening

HOW TO MOLD CHOCOLATES

Flat 8 x 10 inch plastic mold sheets contain small cavity shapes suitable for a variety of special occasions. Molds should be clean and dry before filling with coatings. *Do not grease.* After each using, wipe the mold clean using a paper towel. When finished with the mold wash it in hot water. Detergent may crack the mold. To make solid molded candy pieces, melt the candy coatings (p11) and use a teaspoon to fill the cavities in the mold sheet. Tap mold on table to release air bubbles and level coatings. Chill in freezer for ten minutes to harden and set. Remove from freezer. Turn mold upside down and candy will fall out. If candy does not fall out return to freezer for a few more minutes.

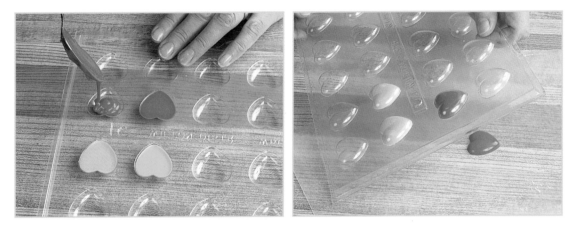

HOW TO PAINT WITH COLORED COATINGS

Many molds have a design in the mold. Using a good quality paint brush, paint directly on the design on the mold. Apply enough melted coatings (p11) so that you do not see light through the color. Use a separate paint brush for each color. When any two colors intersect the color coating underneath must be allowed to set at room temperture (a few minutes) before painting another color over it. The mold can then be filled with chocolate or other colored coatings. Follow directions for how to mold, p12 above. Painted design will be on the chocolates when they are turned out of the mold.

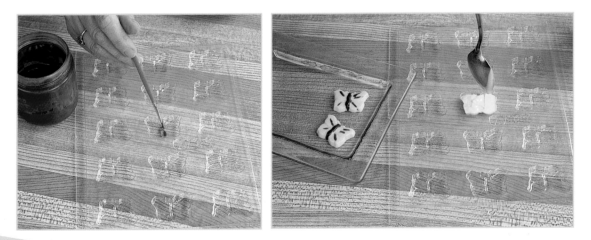

HOW TO GARNISH WITH CHOCOLATE

Chocolate shavings can be made by pulling a vegetable peeler along the edge of a milk chocolate candy bar at room temperature. Grated chocolate sprinkles are made using any kind of hard chocolate and a hand grater. Chocolate curls need 4 ounces of semi-sweet chocolate, melted (p11). Pour onto a wax-paper-lined cookie sheet and spread into 3-inch-wide strips. Chill in a refrigerator until almost firm. Remove. Slowly pull the vegetable peeler across the chocolate strip and transfer the curls with a toothpick to the candy.

HOW TO COLOR COATINGS

Use a bit of paste food coloring on the end of a toothpick. These food colorings are concentrated and do not add liquid to your mixture, but make pastel shades only. For more intense colors use colored coatings.

NOTE Too much paste color added to wafers will make the wafers thicken and taste bitter.

HOW TO FLAVOR COATINGS

Add a few drops of oil food flavoring to melted coatings. Flavors are concentrated so do not add too much. Use one drop of oil flavoring to one pound of wafers. Use peppermint or almond for white coatings; orange for orange coatings; cinnamon, cherry, or strawberry for red coatings; lime, spearmint, or wintergreen for green coatings; lemon, banana, or pineapple for yellow coatings.

NOTE Do not use extracts to flavor coatings. They add too much liquid making the coatings unsuitable for molding.

STORING CHOCOLATE OR COATINGS

Store chocolate or coatings in a cool, dry place where temperatures range between 65°F and 70°F. Do not freeze or store in refrigerator. Coatings will pick up moisture making them difficult to melt.

STORAGE TIMES FOR CANDIES

Store all candies in a cool, dry place in airtight containers. The harder the candy, the longer it will store.

TRUFFLES	2 to 3 days	JELLIES	2 weeks	FUDGE	3 to 4 weeks
CARAMELS	10 to 14 days	NUTTY CANDIES	2 weeks	NOUGATS	3 to 4 weeks
CHOCOLATES	14 days	FONDANT, COOKED	6 months	MARZIPAN	3 to 4 weeks
TOFFEE	2 weeks	FONDANT, UNCOOKED	Use immediately		

HOW TO PREPARE BRITTLE

To spread brittle thinly and evenly, pour cooked mixture onto a buttered cookie sheet. Quickly use the back of a wooden spoon to spread mixture to the edges of the pan. Use 2 forks to stretch and lift the mixture to a thin even sheet.

Thrifty Make-at-Home Basics

The following two items are used very often in candy making. You can make them at home and always have them at hand.

HOW TO MAKE MARSHMALLOWS

Marshmallows are used very often in candy making. Here's an economical recipe to make your own. They're also delicious to eat by themselves or use as a filling for chocolate shells or Easter eggs.

14

Homemade Marshmallows

powdered sugar (see p8) for dusting
2 tablespoons gelatin
8 tablespoons cold water
2 cups granulated sugar
1/2 cup cold water
1/4 teaspoon salt
2 teaspoons vanilla extract

1 Dust a 8-inch or 9-inch square pan thickly with powdered sugar. Set aside.

2 In a small bowl, soak gelatin in 8 tablespoons of cold water. Set aside.

3 Combine granulated sugar and 1/2 cup of water in a large heavy saucepan.

4 Cook and stir over MEDIUM heat until dissolved. Add gelatin and bring to a boil.

5 Remove from heat. Pour into a large bowl and let stand until partially cool.

6 Add salt and vanilla extract. Beat with an electric mixer until soft and double in volume.

7 Pour into the prepared pan to about 1/2 inch thick.

8 Set to cool until it will not stick to the finger.

9 Cut in1-1/2 inch pieces and roll in powdered sugar. (Cut in 3/4 inch pieces for miniature marshmallows.)

NOTE Toasted coconut can be substituted for powdered sugar.

HOW TO MAKE SWEETENED CONDENSED MILK
This is a simple recipe that works well every time.

Homemade Sweetened Condensed Milk

1 cup instant dry nonfat milk
2/3 cup granulated sugar
1/3 cup boiling water
1/4 cup butter, melted

1 Combine all ingredients in a blender and blend until smooth. Scrape down the sides of the blender 2 or 3 times. Store this milk up to 5 days in the refrigerator.

Makes 1 cup

Nutty Buttermilk Fudge

2 cups granulated sugar
1 tablespoon light corn syrup
1 cup buttermilk
1 teaspoon baking soda
1/8 teaspoon salt
1/2 cup butter
1 teaspoon vanilla extract
1 to 2 cups pecans or walnuts, chopped

1 Butter an 8-inch square pan. Set aside.

2 Combine the sugar, corn syrup, buttermilk, baking soda, and salt in a *very large*, heavy saucepan (to accommodate the foaming action of soda and buttermilk).

3 Cook and stir constantly over MEDIUM heat, washing down sides of pan frequently with a pastry brush dipped in hot water to remove sugar crystals. Cook until sugar is dissolved and mixture comes to a boil. Add the butter and a candy thermometer.

4 Continue to cook over MEDIUM heat, stirring often until candy thermometer reaches 238°F (soft ball stage, p10). Remove from heat.

5 Cool without stirring until lukewarm—110°F.

6 Add vanilla extract and beat vigorously with a wooden spoon until mixture begins to thicken and lose its gloss.

7 Stir in nuts and quickly spread in the prepared pan.

8 Cool until firm and cut into squares. Store in the refrigerator covered with plastic wrap.

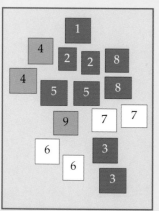

Chocolate-Maple Layered Fudge

1. Make Maple Cream Fudge (p22) replacing walnuts with 1/2 cup glazed cherries. Allow to set.
2. Make Rich Chocolate Fudge (p19), adding 1/2 cup chopped walnuts.
3. Pour the Rich Chocolate Fudge over the set Maple Cream Fudge. Score into squares with a knife. Refrigerate until firm.
4. Cut into squares. Store in the refrigerator covered with plastic wrap.

Macadamia Nut Fudge

8 tablespoons butter, cut in pieces
1 cup semi-sweet chocolate chips
1 cup macadamia nuts, coarsely chopped
1 ounce unsweetened chocolate, finely chopped
1 teaspoon vanilla extract
2-1/4 cups granulated sugar
2/3 cup evaporated milk
12 large marshmallows

1. Butter an 8-inch square pan. Line the bottom of the pan with foil.
2. Combine the butter, chocolate chips, macadamia nuts, unsweetened chocolate, and vanilla extract in a large bowl.
3. Combine the sugar, evaporated milk, and marshmallows in a medium-size saucepan. Cook and stir mixture over MEDIUM heat, until sugar is disolved. Wash down sides of pan frequently with a pastry brush dipped in hot water to remove sugar crystals. Add a candy thermometer.
4. Cook, stirring constantly, until mixture comes to a boil. Continue to cook, stirring constantly, until mixture reaches 238°F (soft ball stage, p10).
5. Remove from heat. Pour heated mixture into the chocolate chip-macadamia nut bowl and allow to stand for 30 minutes. Stir until mixture begins to thicken, about 1 minute.
6. Spread evenly into the prepared baking pan and allow to cool completely. Cover with foil and let stand overnight to allow flavors to blend.
7. Invert the pan and remove pan-lined foil. Reinvert fudge and cut into squares.
8. Store in an airtight container at room temperature.

Rich Chocolate Fudge

1 cup granulated sugar
1 cup brown sugar
1/4 cup light corn syrup
1/2 cup milk
1/4 cup butter, melted
2 tablespoons cocoa powder
1 teaspoon vanilla extract

1 Butter an 8-inch square pan. Set aside.

2 Combine the sugars, syrup, milk, and melted butter in a large, heavy saucepan. Boil 2-1/2 minutes, then add the cocoa powder and stir.

3 Cook and stir over MEDIUM heat until mixture comes to a boil. Wash down sides of pan frequently with a pastry brush dipped in hot water to remove sugar crystals. Add a candy thermometer.

4 Boil 5 minutes, to 238°F, (soft ball stage, p10), stirring occasionally. Remove from heat and add vanilla extract. Allow to cool 5 minutes.

5 Beat with a wooden spoon until creamy.

6 Pour into the prepared pan. Score into squares with a knife. Refrigerate until firm.

7 Cut into squares and store in the refrigerator covered with plastic wrap.

Easy No-Cook White Fudge

1 pound vanilla-flavored candy coatings
7 ounces marshmallow creme
1/4 cup butter
2/3 cup sweetened condensed milk
1/2 cup shredded coconut
1 cup pecans, chopped

1 Line an 8-inch square pan with foil. Set aside.

2 Melt the candy coatings (p11).

3 Combine the marshmallow creme, butter, sweetened condensed milk, coconut, and pecans. Stir into the melted candy coatings.

4 Spread in the prepared pan. Cool completely. Cut into squares with a knife.

5 Store in a tightly covered container at room temperature.

NOTE For Valentines's Day centerpieces for the table, pour hot fudge into heart-shaped pans.

Nut Penuche

2-1/4 cups light brown sugar, firmly packed
3/4 cup light cream, (half & half)
1/8 teaspoon salt
2-1/2 tablespoons butter or margarine
1 teaspoon vanilla extract
1/2 cup walnuts or pecans, chopped

1. Butter an 8-inch square pan. Set aside.
2. Combine the sugar, light cream, and salt in a large heavy saucepan.
3. Cook and stir over MEDIUM heat until sugar dissolves. Cook until mixture comes to a boil. Wash down sides of pan frequently with a pastry brush dipped in hot water to remove sugar crystals. Add a candy thermometer.
4. Cook without stirring until mixture reaches 238°F (soft ball stage, p10). Remove from heat.
5. Add butter without stirring. Cool to lukewarm (110°F).
6. Add vanilla extract and beat with a wooden spoon until mixture begins to thicken.
7. Add the nuts and beat until thick and creamy.
8. Pour at once into the prepared pan and score into squares with a knife.
9. Cool completely and cut into squares. Store in the refrigerator covered with plastic wrap.

Extra Creamy Fudge

2 cups brown sugar
3 tablespoons all purpose flour
2 tablespoons butter
1/2 cup milk
1/4 teaspoon salt
1-1/2 teaspoons baking powder
1 teaspoon vanilla extract
1/2 cup walnuts, chopped

1. Butter an 8-inch square pan. Set aside.
2. Combine the sugar, flour, butter, milk, salt, and baking powder in a large heavy saucepan.
3. Cook and stir mixture over MEDIUM heat, until sugar dissolves. Cook until mixture comes to a boil. Wash down sides of pan frequently with a pastry brush dipped in hot water to remove sugar crystals. Add a candy thermometer.
4. Cook over MEDIUM heat, stirring occasionally, to 238°F (soft ball stage, p10), about 30 minutes. Remove from heat. Add vanilla extract.
5. Cool slightly. Add the walnuts. Beat until creamy with a wooden spoon.
6. Pour into the prepared pan. Score into squares with a knife.
7. Cool completely and cut into squares. Store in the refrigerator covered with plastic wrap.

Caramel Fudge Fantasy

2 cups granulated sugar
6 ounces evaporated milk
2 tablespoons light corn syrup
10 ounces caramel sauce (ice-cream topping)
1 teaspoon vanilla extract
1/4 teaspoon maple extract
1/2 cup walnuts, chopped

1 Butter an 8-inch square pan. Set aside.

2 Combine the sugar, evaporated milk, corn syrup, and caramel sauce in a large heavy saucepan.

3 Cook and stir mixture over MEDIUM heat until sugar dissolves, washing down the sides of the pan frequently with a pastry brush dipped in hot water to remove sugar crystals. Cook until mixture comes to a boil. Add a candy thermometer.

4 Cook to 238°F (soft ball stage, p10), stirring occasionally. Remove from heat.

5 Stir in vanilla and maple extracts.

6 Beat with a wooden spoon just until mixture begins to lose its gloss. Stir in the walnuts.

7 Pour into the prepared pan. Cut into squares when firm. Store in the refrigerator covered with plastic wrap.

Almond Fudge Squares

2 tablespoons butter
2/3 cup evaporated milk
1-2/3 cups granulated sugar
1/2 teaspoon salt
2 cups mini-marshmallows
1-1/2 cups semi-sweet chocolate chips
1/2 cup almonds, chopped
1/4 teaspoon almond extract

1 Butter a 9-inch square pan. Set aside.

2 Combine the butter, evaporated milk, sugar, and salt in a large heavy saucepan.

3 Cook and stir over MEDIUM heat until sugar dissolves, washing down sides of pan frequently with a pastry brush dipped in hot water to remove sugar crystals. Cook until mixture comes to a boil. Add a candy thermometer.

4 Cook over MEDIUM heat, stirring occasionally, to 238°F (soft ball stage, p10), about 30 minutes.

5 Remove from heat. Stir in the marshmallows, chocolate chips, almonds, and almond extract.

6 Continue stirring until marshmallows and chocolate chips are completely melted.

7 Pour into the prepared pan. Score into squares using a knife.

8 Cool completely. Cut into squares. Store in the refrigerator covered with plastic wrap.

Piña Colada Fudge

2 pounds yellow or white vanilla-flavored candy coatings
1/2 cup butter or margarine
1 teaspoon rum-butter extract
1 teaspoon pineapple extract
1-1/2 cups marshmallow creme
1-1/2 cups nuts
1 cup coconut
14 ounces sweetened condensed milk

1 Line a 10-inch square pan with foil. Set aside.

2 Melt the candy coatings (p11) and stir in the remaining ingredients.

3 Pour into the prepared pan.

4 Score into squares with a knife. Cover the top of the pan with foil and allow to set overnight.

5 Cut fudge in squares and store in an airtight container.

NOTE For a smaller batch, this recipe can be cut in half successfuly.

1 *Piña Colada Fudge, p22*
2 *Maple Cream Fudge, p22*
3 *Easy White Fudge, p24*
4 *Never Fail Chocolate Fudge, p24*
5 *Layered Peppermint Fudge, p25*

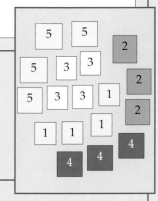

Maple Cream Fudge

1/2 cup butter
2 cups brown sugar
5 tablespoons evaporated milk
1 cup powdered sugar (see p8)
1 teaspoon vanilla extract
1/2 cup walnuts, chopped

1 Butter an 8-inch square pan. Set aside.

2 Combine the butter, brown sugar, and milk in a large, heavy saucepan.

3 Cook and stir over MEDIUM heat until mixture comes to a boil. Wash down sides of pan frequently with a pastry brush dipped in hot water to remove sugar crystals. Add a candy thermometer.

4 Cook, stirring occasionally, to 238°F (soft ball stage, p10). Remove from heat.

5 Add powdered sugar and beat with a wooden spoon. Add vanilla extract and the walnuts.

6 Pour into the prepared pan. Score into squares with a knife. Refrigerate until firm.

7 Cut into squares. Store in the refrigerator covered with plastic wrap.

Easy White Fudge

2 cups granulated sugar
2/3 cup sweetened condensed milk
2/3 cup buttermilk
2 tablespoons butter
8 ounces white chocolate, coarsely chopped
1-1/2 cups mini-marshmallows
2 cups nuts, chopped

1 Butter an 9-inch square pan. Set aside.

2 Combine the sugar, sweetened condensed milk, and buttermilk in a large heavy saucepan.

3 Cook and stir over MEDIUM heat until mixture comes to a boil. Wash down sides of pan frequently with a pastry brush dipped in hot water to remove sugar crystals. Add a candy thermometer.

4 Boil 7 minutes, to 238°F (soft ball stage, p10), stirring constantly. Remove from heat.

5 Add the butter, white chocolate, and marshmallows. Stir until smooth.

6 Add nuts. Pour into the prepared pan.

7 Score into squares with a knife. Refrigerate until firm.

8 Cut into squares. Store in the refrigerator covered with plastic wrap.

Never-Fail Chocolate Fudge

1 cup evaporated milk
1 cup butter
2 cups granulated sugar
2 cups brown sugar
1/4 cup cocoa powder
1/2 cup all purpose flour
1 teaspoon vanilla extract

1 Butter a 9-inch square pan. Set aside.

2 Combine the evaporated milk, butter, sugars, and cocoa powder in a large heavy saucepan.

3 Cook over MEDIUM heat, stirring constantly. Wash down the sides of pan frequently with a pastry brush dipped in hot water to remove sugar crystals. Cook until sugars dissolve and mixture comes to a boil. Add a candy thermometer.

4 Boil for 10 minutes, to 238°F (soft ball stage, p10), stirring occasionally.

5 Remove from heat. Add flour and vanilla extract. Mix well with an electric mixer or a wooden spoon.

6 Pour into the prepared pan. Cut into squares immediately.

7 Allow to set completely. Store in the refrigerator covered with plastic wrap.

Layered Cream Cheese Peppermint Fudge

LAYER 1
1/4 cup cream cheese
2 cups powdered sugar (see p8)
2-1/2 tablespoons cocoa powder
1/2 teaspoon vanilla extract
1 teaspoon milk
1/3 cup walnuts, toasted and chopped

1 Butter an 8-inch square pan. Set aside.

2 In a large bowl beat the cream cheese with an electric mixer until softened.

3 Gradually beat in the powdered sugar, cocoa powder, vanilla extract, milk, and walnuts.

4 Press into the prepared pan. Chill in the refrigerator.

LAYER 2
1/4 cup cream cheese
2 cups powdered sugar
1/2 teaspoon mint extract
1 teaspoon milk
1/4 cup peppermint sticks, crushed

5 In a large bowl beat the cream cheese with an electric mixer until softened.

6 Beat in the powdered sugar, mint extract, milk, and crushed peppermint sticks. Beat well.

7 Spread over the chilled chocolate layer and score into squares with a knife.

8 Chill in the refrigerator until firm.

9 Cut into squares. Store in the refrigerator covered with plastic wrap.

Spiced Pumpkin Fudge

3 cups granulated sugar
3/4 cup butter or margarine
2/3 cup evaporated milk
1/2 cup canned pumpkin
1 teaspoon pumpkin pie spice
12 ounces butterscotch chips
7 ounces marshmallow creme
1 cup almonds, chopped and toasted
1 teaspoon vanilla extract

1. Butter a 9 x 13 inch pan. Set aside.
2. Combine the sugar, butter, evaporated milk, pumpkin, and spice in a very large heavy saucepan.
3. Cook and stir mixture over MEDIUM heat until sugar is dissolved, washing down the sides of pan frequently with a pastry brush dipped in hot water to remove sugar crystals. Continue to cook until mixture comes to a boil, stirring constantly. Add a candy thermometer.
4. Continue boiling, stirring constantly, over MEDIUM heat, to 238°F (soft ball stage, p10), about 10 minutes.
5. Remove from heat and add the butterscotch chips. Stir until melted.
6. Add the marshmallow creme, almonds, and vanilla extract, mixing until well blended.
7. Quickly pour into the prepared pan.
8. Cool at room temperature and cut into squares. Store in a tighty covered container in the refrigerator.

Easy Microwave Fudge

4 cups dark- or milk-chocolate-flavored candy coatings
14 ounces sweetened condensed milk
1 cup nuts, chopped (optional)
1-1/2 teaspoons vanilla extract

1. Line a 9-inch square pan with wax paper. Set aside.
2. Combine candy coatings and sweetened condensed milk in a large glass measuring cup.
3. Place in the microwave and cook on DEFROST power 4 to 5 minutes. Stir twice, until melted and smooth.
4. Stir in the nuts and vanilla extract. Spread evenly in the prepared pan.
5. Chill 2 hours in the refrigerator until firm.
6. Turn fudge onto a cutting board. Peel off wax paper and cut fudge into squares with a knife.
7. Store in a tightly covered container at room temperature.

1 *Spiced Pumpkin Fudge, p26*
2 *Easy Microwave Fudge, p26*
3 *Stacked Fudge, p28*
4 *Sweet & Sour Fudge, p28*

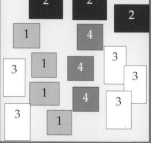

27

Stacked Fudge

CHOCOLATE MOCHA LAYER
6 ounces chocolate chips
1 teaspoon vanilla extract
1 teaspoon instant coffee
1/3 cup sweetened condensed milk

BUTTERSCOTCH LAYER
6 ounces butterscotch chips
1/3 cup sweetened condensed milk
1 teaspoon vanilla extract

1. Butter 2—8-inch square pans. Set aside.
2. Melt the chocolate chips (p11). Add the vanilla extract, coffee, and sweetened condensed milk.
3. Spread in one of the prepared pans. Chill in the refrigerator.
4. Melt the butterscotch chips, as above.
5. Stir in the milk and vanilla extract. Pour into the second prepared pan. Chill in the refrigerator.
6. Cut each pan of candy into 6 strips. Stack alternately.
7. Wrap each stacked bar in plastic wrap and refrigerate.
8. To serve, cut the bars into thin slices with a sharp knife. Store in the refrigerator covered with plastic wrap.

Sweet & Sour Fudge

2 cups brown sugar
1 cup sour cream
4 tablespoons light corn syrup
1/8 teaspoon salt
6 tablespoons cocoa powder
1 teaspoon vanilla extract

1. Butter an 8-inch square pan. Set aside.
2. Combine the sugar, sour cream, corn syrup, salt, and cocoa powder in a large heavy saucepan.
3. Cook and stir the mixture over MEDIUM heat, until the sugar dissolves. Wash down sides of pan frequently with a pastry brush dipped in hot water to remove sugar crystals. Cook until mixture comes to a boil. Add a candy thermometer.
4. Continue cooking mixture over LOW to MEDIUM heat, stirring occasionally, to 238°F (soft ball stage, p10). Remove from heat.
5. Add vanilla extract and beat with a wooden spoon until creamy.
6. Pour into the prepared pan. Score into squares with a knife.
7. Cool fudge completely. Cut into squares. Store in the refrigerator covered with plastic wrap.

Butter Caramels

1/2 cup nuts, finely chopped
2 cups granulated sugar
1/4 cup light corn syrup
1/2 cup butter
2 cups light cream (half & half)

1 Butter an 8-inch square pan. Spread nuts in the pan. Set aside.

2 Combine the sugar, corn syrup, butter, and 1 cup of light cream in a large heavy saucepan.

3 Heat to boiling over MEDIUM heat, stirring constantly. Wash down sides of pan frequently with a pastry brush dipped in hot water to remove sugar crystals. Stir in the remaining cup of light cream. Add a candy thermometer.

4 Cook over MEDIUM heat, stirring occasionally, to 246°F (firm ball stage, p10). Immediately spread mixture evenly over nuts in the pan. Cool.

5 Cut into 1 inch squares with a knife. Store in the refrigerator covered with plastic wrap.

NOTE Use soft caramel (soft ball stage, p10) as a filling for turtles or chocolates made in a mold.

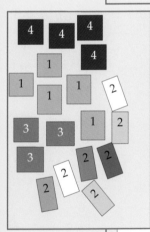

Photograph, p29
1 *Butter Caramels, p30*
2 *Microwave Caramels, p30*
3 *Coffee Caramels, p31*
4 *Chocolate Caramels, p31*

Microwave Caramels

1 cup butter or margarine
2-1/4 cups brown sugar
1 cup light corn syrup
14 ounces sweetened condensed milk
1/8 teaspoon salt
1 teaspoon vanilla extract

1 Butter a 9-inch square pan. Set aside.

2 Put the butter in a large microwave-safe bowl and microwave at MEDIUM HIGH for 1 to 2 minutes to melt.

3 Blend in the sugar, corn syrup, sweetened condensed milk, and salt. Cover with plastic wrap. Microwave at HIGH for 7 minutes, until mixture comes to a boil. Stir well.

4 Microwave uncovered on MEDIUM HIGH for 13 minutes to 238°F (soft ball stage, p10). Test with a candy thermometer. Remove from the microwave. Stir in the vanilla extract.

5 Pour into the prepared pan. Score with a sharp knife. Cool to room temperature.

6 Cut in squares and twist in colored wrappers. Store in the refrigerator in a covered container.

Coffee Caramels

1 cup granulated sugar
1/2 cup brown sugar
1/2 cup light corn syrup
1-1/2 cups light cream (half & half)
2 tablespoons instant coffee
1/4 cup butter
1 teaspoon vanilla extract

1 Line an 8-inch square pan with foil and butter lightly. Set aside.

2 Combine the sugars, corn syrup, light cream, instant coffee, and butter in a large heavy saucepan.

3 Cook, stirring constantly, over LOW heat until the sugars are dissolved. Wash down the sides of pan frequently with a pastry brush dipped in hot water to remove sugar crystals. Continue cooking over MEDIUM heat until the mixture comes to a boil. Add a candy thermometer.

4 Cook over MEDIUM heat, stirring occasionally, to 246°F (firm ball stage, p10).

5 Remove from heat and stir in the vanilla extract. Pour into the prepared pan. Score while still warm.

6 When cool cut in squares with a knife. Store in the refrigerator covered with plastic wrap.

Chocolate Caramels

1 cup butter or margarine
2-1/4 cups brown sugar
1/8 teaspoon salt
1 cup light corn syrup
14 ounces sweetened condensed milk
2—1 ounce squares unsweetened chocolate
1 teaspoon vanilla extract

1 Butter a 9-inch square pan. Set aside.

2 Melt the butter in a very large heavy saucepan over MEDIUM heat.

3 Add the sugar and salt. Stir thoroughly. Stir in the corn syrup.

4 Gradually add the sweetened condensed milk, followed by unsweetened chocolate.

5 Add a candy thermometer. Cook and stir mixture over MEDIUM heat. Wash down the sides of pan frequently with a pastry brush dipped in hot water to remove sugar crystals.

6 Cook to 246°F (firm ball stage, p10), about 15 minutes.

7 Remove from heat and stir in the vanilla extract.

8 Pour into the prepared pan. Score while still warm. Cool and cut into squares. Store in the refrigerator covered with plastic wrap.

NOTE If you prefer plain caramels, simply omit the unsweetened chocolate.

No-Cook Fondant Chocolates

1/2 cup butter
7-1/2 to 8 cups powdered sugar (see p8)
14 ounces sweetened condensed milk
1 teaspoon vanilla extract
1/4 teaspoon salt
nuts, coconut, candied fruits (optional)
paste food coloring (optional)
2 pounds chocolate-flavored coatings

1 Line a cookie sheet with wax paper. Set aside.

2 Combine the butter, 4 cups powdered sugar, and sweetened condensed milk in a large bowl. Mix well. Add the vanilla extract and salt.

3 Add remaining powdered sugar gradually with a wooden spoon. Knead mixture to blend.

4 Add nuts, coconut, candied fruit, and paste food coloring of your choice.

5 With clean buttered hands, form dough into small balls and place on the prepared pan. Allow to set several hours.

6 Using a dipping spoon, dip (p11) these centers in melted chocolate-flavored coatings (p11) or colored coatings of your choice. Place on the cookie sheet. Allow to set at room temperature.

NOTE Fondant can be divided into 3 or 4 portions and each one colored and flavored differently.

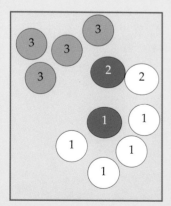

Photograph on page 32
1 *No-Cook Fondant Chocolates, p33*
2 *Peanut Butter Fondant Chocolates, p34*
3 *Pecan Rolls, p34*

Peanut Butter Fondant Chocolates

2 cups crunchy peanut butter
1/2 cup butter
4 cups powdered sugar (see p8)
3 cups rice crispy cereal
4 cups chocolate-flavored candy coatings for dipping

1 Line a cookie sheet with wax paper. Set aside.

2 Combine the crunchy peanut butter, butter, and powdered sugar in a large bowl.

3 Add rice crispy cereal and blend well. With your hands, form the dough into 3/4 inch balls and set on the cookie sheet for several hours.

4 Melt coatings (p11) and dip centers (p11), using a dipping spoon. Place on the prepared cookie sheet to set, at room temperature.

Pecan Rolls

1/4 cup light corn syrup
1/4 cup water
1-1/4 cups granulated sugar
1 egg white
1/8 teaspoon cream of tartar
1 teaspoon vanilla extract
14 ounces caramels
3 tablespoons water
2 cups pecans, coarsely chopped

1 Line a 9 x 5 inch loaf pan with buttered wax paper. Line a large cookie sheet with wax paper and spread pecans on this sheet. Set aside.

2 Combine the corn syrup, water, and sugar in a small heavy saucepan.

3 Cook, stirring constantly, over MEDIUM heat, washing down sides of pan frequently with a pastry brush dipped in hot water to remove sugar crystals. Cook until the mixture comes to a boil and the sugar dissolves. Add a candy thermometer.

4 Continue to cook over MEDIUM heat to 258°F (hard ball stage, p10).

5 Beat the egg white and cream of tartar with an electric mixer until stiff but not dry.

6 Slowly pour the hot syrup into the egg white, beating constantly.

7 Add vanilla extract and beat until mixture forms soft peaks and starts to lose its gloss.

8 Spoon fondant into the prepared loaf pan. Cut in 3 strips lengthwise, then crosswise in the center. Freeze until firm.

9 Melt the caramels and water in a small heavy saucepan over LOW heat, stirring occasionally.

10 Working quickly, drop each piece of frozen fondant into the melted caramel. When completely coated, roll in the pecans. Allow to set. (Reheat caramel if mixture becomes too thick).

11 Wrap and store in the refrigerator in airtight container, or freeze up to 3 months.

Easy Cooked Fondant

1/2 cup light corn syrup
1/2 cup butter or margarine
4 cups powdered sugar, sifted (see p8)
1 teaspoon vanilla extract
paste food coloring (optional)

1 Butter an 8-inch square pan. Set aside.

2 Combine the corn syrup, butter, and 2 cups of powdered sugar in a medium-size heavy saucepan.

3 Cook, stirring constantly, over MEDIUM heat. Cook until mixture comes to a boil. Remove from the heat.

4 Stir in the remaining 2 cups of sifted powdered sugar, one cup at a time, stirring well after each cup to dissolve the sugar. Add the vanilla extract. Pour mixture into the prepared pan. Allow to cool.

5 Knead in paste food coloring, a little at a time. If you divide fondant, color each portion separately. Shape in balls. Store in refrigerator.

Raspberry Truffles

16 ounces semi-sweet chocolate chips
1/4 cup whipping cream
1 tablespoon butter
1/4 cup seedless raspberry preserves
1 teaspoon vanilla extract
walnuts, finely chopped
cocoa powder for rolling
1 cup chocolate-flavored candy coatings (coats about 12 truffles)
24 paper candy cups

1 Line 2 cookie sheets with wax paper. Set aside.

2 Combine the chocolate chips, whipping cream, and butter in a large microwave-safe bowl.

3 Cover with wax paper and microwave on MEDIUM HIGH for 1-1/2 to 2-1/2 minutes. *Do not boil.* Stir. Let stand 1 minute.

4 In another microwave-safe bowl, heat raspberry preserves on MEDIUM for 20 to 30 seconds until warm. Remove from the microwave.

5 Add the warmed preserves and vanilla extract to the chocolate mixture and whisk until smooth.

6 Cover chocolate mixture with plastic wrap, pressing wrap directly onto the surface of the chocolate. Cool. Refrigerate for 1-1/2 to 2 hours or freeze for 35 to 45 minutes until firm enough to scoop and roll into balls. DO NOT COMPLETELY FREEZE.

7 Place the walnuts and cocoa powder in separate bowls.

8 Using a teaspoon, scoop mixture and roll into 1 inch balls between the palms of your hands. Set on cookie sheet. If mixture becomes too soft to roll return to the freezer until firm.

9 Divide truffles, placing truffles that will be coated in chocolate on the other cookie sheet and freeze until firm (about 30 minutes).

10 Roll other truffles in walnuts or cocoa powder shaking off excess cocoa. Place each rolled truffle in a paper candy cup.

11 In a microwave-safe bowl heat chocolate-flavored coatings in microwave on DEFROST for 2 to 3 minutes, stirring twice.

12 To keep chocolate from setting, place the bowl of melted chocolate over a bowl of warm water or return to the microwave.

13 Using a dipping spoon, dip each frozen truffle into melted chocolate letting excess chocolate drip off (p11). Place on second prepared cookie sheet. Chill until firm. Place in paper candy cups.

14 Store in the refrigerator in an airtight container for 5 days. Let truffles stand at room temperature for about 10 minutes before serving. Truffles may be frozen for up to 1 month. Thaw overnight in the refrigerator, then at room temperature before serving.

Chocolate Truffles

1/4 cup butter
1/2 cup whipping cream
3 tablespoons granulated sugar
1-1/3 cups semi-sweet chocolate, chopped
1/4 cup cream liqueur
grated chocolate, coconut, chocolate sprinkles, cocoa powder,
powdered sugar, chocolate-flavored coatings (finely chopped),
nuts (finely chopped), for covering

1 Line a cookie sheet with wax paper. Set aside.

2 Combine the butter, whipping cream, and sugar in a medium-size heavy saucepan and stir over MEDIUM heat. Bring to a boil. Remove from heat.

3 Add the semi-sweet chocolate and stir until dissolved completely. Add the liqueur.

4 Chill the mixture in the refrigerator overnight.

5 Shape mixture into balls by teaspoonfuls and roll in one of the coverings. Repeat using various coverings.

Peppermint Truffles

4 ounces semi-sweet-chocolate-flavored coatings
4 ounces milk chocolate
1 teaspoon peppermint extract
1/3 cup unsalted butter (at room temperature)
1/2 cup ground peppermint candy cane
1 pound dark-chocolate-flavored coatings for dipping

1 Line a cookie sheet with wax paper. Set aside.

2 Melt semi-sweet-chocolate-flavored coatings and milk chocolate in a double boiler (p11).

3 Add peppermint extract and stir well.

4 With an electric mixer on HIGH, beat butter into the warm chocolate until light and fluffy.

5 Fold in ground peppermint candy cane. Chill until mixture is firm (1 to 3 hours).

6 Using a melon scoop make 1 inch balls and place on the prepared pan. Cover with plastic wrap and freeze until firm.

7 Using a dipping spoon, dip frozen balls (p11) in melted (p11) dark-chocolate-flavored coatings.

8 Sprinkle with crushed peppermint.

9 Store in the refrigerator in a covered container up to 1 month or in a freezer for 3 months.

Bittersweet Cocoa Truffles

1/2 cup butter or margarine
3/4 cup cocoa powder
14 ounces sweetened condensed milk
1 teaspoon vanilla extract
2 tablespoons cocoa powder, for rolling

1 Butter an 8-inch square pan. Set aside.

2 Melt the butter in a heavy saucepan over LOW heat. Stir in the cocoa powder.

3 Slowly add sweetened condensed milk, stirring constantly until smooth.

4 Cook over MEDIUM heat, stirring constantly, until thickened and smooth (about 3 minutes).

5 Remove from heat and add vanilla extract.

6 Pour the mixture into the prepared pan. Cover and chill in the refrigerator until firm.

7 Remove from refrigerator. Shape into 1-1/4 inch balls and roll them in additional cocoa powder.

8 Place balls in small paper baking cups. Store in an airtight container in the refrigerator.

1 *White Chocolate Truffles, p41*
2 *Bittersweet Cocoa Truffles, p39*
3 *Peppermint Truffles, p38*
4 *Minty Chocolate Truffles, p40*
5 *Caramel Truffles, p40*
6 *Chocolate Truffles, p38*

Caramel Truffles

8 ounces milk chocolate, chopped
4 tablespoons butter
1/3 cup caramel topping
1 cup pecans, chopped

1 Line a cookie sheet with wax paper. Set aside.

2 Combine the chocolate and butter in a medium-size heavy saucepan and melt (p11) on MEDIUM heat.

3 Remove from heat.

4 Beat in caramel topping with a wooden spoon. Chill for a few minutes, then roll in chopped pecans.

5 Set on wax paper. Chill truffles until firm.

Minty Chocolate Truffles

12 ounces semi-sweet chocolate chips
1/4 cup egg substitute
1/4 cup plus 2 tablespoons butter or margarine, cut in pieces
1/4 cup plus 2 tablespoons sifted powdered sugar (see p8)
1/2 teaspoon mint extract
12 ounces chocolate-flavored candy coatings
2 ounces white vanilla-flavored candy coatings

1 Line a cookie sheet with wax paper. Set aside.

2 Melt chocolate chips in top of a double boiler (p11).

3 Beat egg substitute 1 minute with an electric mixer. Gradually add the melted chocolate, stirring constantly.

4 Add the butter, sifted powdered sugar, and mint extract. Beat at MEDIUM speed with an electric mixer until the mixture is smooth.

5 Cover and chill in the refrigerator for 1 hour.

6 Shape mixture into 1 inch balls, cover and chill in the refrigerator until firm.

7 Melt chocolate candy coatings in top of the double boiler (p11).

8 Using a dipping spoon, dip each ball into coatings (p11) letting excess drip off.

9 Place on the prepared pan and chill until coatings harden.

10 Drizzle truffles with melted (p11) white vanilla-flavored candy coatings.

White Chocolate Truffles

12 ounces white chocolate-flavored candy coatings
1 tablespoon orange, almond, raspberry, or rum extract
(1/4 cup of any flavored liqueur may be substituted for the extract)
1 can vanilla frosting
1 to 2 cups ground nuts, coconut, or powdered sugar
60 foil candy cups

1 Put nuts, or coconut, or powdered sugar in a pie pan to be used as covering. Set aside.

2 Put candy coatings in a microwave-safe bowl or large glass measuring cup and place in the microwave on DEFROST for 5 minutes, stirring every minute until coatings are melted.

3 Stir in extract and frosting. Blend well.

4 Refrigerate 1 to 2 hours until firm.

5 Wash hands and roll mixture into 1 inch balls. Drop balls onto desired coverings (mixture will be sticky). Roll to coat.

6 Place balls in foil candy cups. Store in the refrigerator.

Toffee Crunch

1/2 cup pecans, chopped
3/4 cup brown sugar, packed
1/2 cup butter
6 ounces semi-sweet chocolate chips

1 Butter an 8-inch square pan. Spread pecans in the pan. Set aside.

2 Combine the sugar and butter in a large heavy saucepan.

3 Cook over MEDIUM heat, stirring constantly, until mixture comes to a boil. Wash down sides of pan frequently with a pastry brush dipped in hot water to remove sugar crystals. Add a candy thermometer.

4 Boil to 260°F (hard ball stage, p10), about 7 minutes, stirring constantly.

5 Remove from heat and immediately spread mixture evenly over nuts in the pan.

6 Sprinkle chocolate chips over hot mixture. Place a cookie sheet over the pan to hasten melting. Spread melted chocolate over candy.

7 Chill until firm. Break into pieces

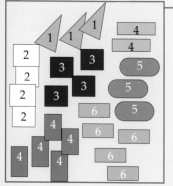

1 *English Toffee, p44*
2 *Sesame Seed Toffee, p44*
3 *Toffee Crunch, p43*
4 *Creamy Toffee, p43*
5 *Old-Fashioned Pull Toffee, p45*
6 *Russian Toffee, p45*

Creamy Toffee

14 ounces sweetened condensed milk
2 cups brown sugar
1/2 pound butter (*do not use margarine*)
1 cup light corn syrup

1 Butter a 9-inch square pan. Set aside.

2 Combine all ingredients in a large heavy saucepan. Cook and stir over MEDIUM heat until sugar is dissolved. Wash down sides of pan frequently with a pastry brush dipped in hot water to remove sugar crystals. Add a candy thermometer.

3 Bring the mixture to a boil. stirring constantly. Continue to stir constantly over LOW heat to 260°F (hard ball stage p10), about 22 minutes. Remove from heat.

4 Pour into the prepared pan. Score while still warm. Allow to set.

5 Cut in squares and twist in colored wrap. Store in the refrigerator.

Sesame Seed Toffee

1 cup sesame seeds
1/4 cup butter
1/2 cup light corn syrup
1 cup granulated sugar
1/2 teaspoon vanilla extract
1/4 teaspoon salt

1 Butter a 9 x 13 inch pan. Set aside.

2 Spread sesame seeds on a cookie sheet and toast in an oven at 350°F for 10 minutes, stirring frequently. Set aside to cool.

3 Melt the butter in a large heavy saucepan over MEDIUM heat. Stir in the corn syrup and sugar. Wash down the sides of pan frequently with a pastry brush dipped in hot water to remove sugar crystals. Add a candy thermometer.

4 Cook on HIGH heat, stirring frequently, to 290°F (soft crack stage, p10).

5 Remove from heat and quickly add the toasted sesame seeds, vanilla extract, and salt.

6 Blend and pour immediately into the prepared pan. Shake pan to help spread the candy evenly.

7 Allow to stand until cool and hard. Break into bite-size pieces.

8 Store in an airtight container.

English Toffee

3/4 pound butter
1/3 cup water
2 cups granulated sugar
1/4 teaspoon salt
2/3 cup almonds, skins on, chopped

1 Lightly butter a jelly roll pan. Set aside.

2 Melt butter in a large heavy saucepan over MEDIUM heat.

3 Add the water, sugar, and salt and cook over MEDIUM heat, stirring constantly. Wash down sides of pan frequently with a pastry brush dipped in hot water to remove sugar crystals.

4 Cook to 258°F (hard ball stage, p10), then add the almonds.

5 Continue to cook and stir to 310°F (hard crack stage, p10). Syrup should be golden brown.

6 Pour candy into the prepared pan. When candy is pliable, score into bite-size pieces.

7 Cool completely. Break candy apart.

Russian Toffee

1/2 pound butter
14 ounces sweetened condensed milk
1 cup light corn syrup
2 cups brown sugar
3/4 cups nuts, chopped

1 Butter an 8 x 11 inch pan. Set aside.

2 Combine the butter, sweetened condensed milk, corn syrup, and sugar in a large heavy saucepan.

3 Cook and stir over MEDIUM heat. Wash down sides of pan frequently with a pastry brush dipped in hot water to remove sugar crystals. Add a candy thermometer.

4 Cook to 260°F (hard ball stage, p10), about 1/2 hour, stirring constantly.

5 Add nuts and pour into the prepared pan.

6 Score and cut into small pieces. Allow to set.

7 Twist pieces into colored wrap.

Old-Fashioned Pull Toffee

1/2 cup molasses
1-1/2 cups granulated sugar
1/2 cup water
1-1/2 tablespoons vinegar
1/4 teaspoon cream of tartar
1/2 cup butter, melted
1/8 teaspoon baking soda

1 Butter an 8-inch square pan. Set aside.

2 Combine the molasses, sugar, water, and vinegar in a large heavy saucepan.

3 Cook and stir constantly over MEDIUM heat until mixture comes to a boil. Add cream of tartar. Wash down sides of pan frequently with a pastry brush dipped in hot water to remove sugar crystals. Add a candy thermometer.

4 Continue cooking without stirring to 300° to 308°F (hard crack stage, p10).

5 Add melted butter and baking soda. Cook one minute longer.

6 Pour into the prepared pan. Cool 10 minutes.

7 Butter hands and pull taffy until porous and cream colored.

8 Shape into a long rope-twisted strand. Cut into 1-inch crosswise pieces with a knife or scissors.

9 Cool, then chill in the refrigerator.

Divinity Sea Foam

3 cups granulated sugar
1/2 cup light corn syrup
1/ 8 teaspoon salt
2/3 cup water
2 egg whites
1 teaspoon vanilla extract
1 cup pecans, coarsely chopped

1 Line a cookie sheet with wax paper. Set aside.

2 Combine the sugar, corn syrup, salt, and water in a large heavy saucepan.

3 Cook over MEDIUM heat, stirring constantly, until sugar dissolves and mixture comes to a boil. Wash down sides of pan frequently with a pastry brush dipped in hot water to remove sugar crystals. Add a candy thermometer.

4 Cook without stirring to 250°F to 260°F (hard ball stage, p10).

5 Beat egg whites with an electric mixer in a large bowl until stiff.

6 Pour the cooked syrup slowly into the beaten whites, beating constantly at HIGH speed until the mixture loses its gloss and forms soft peaks (about 10 minutes).

7 Add vanilla extract and pecans. Mix until well blended.

8 Drop by teaspoonfuls onto wax paper. Cool to set.

NOTE For variety try orange, lemon, almond, or peppermint flavoring and candied lemon or orange peel or coconut in place of the pecans.

Surprise Drops

2 cups granulated sugar
2/3 cup milk
1 cup soda cracker crumbs, finely ground
1/2 cup almonds or pecans, toasted, finely chopped
1 teaspoon vanilla extract
1/2 cup crunchy peanut butter

1 Line a cookie sheet with wax paper. Set aside.

2 Combine the sugar and milk in a large heavy saucepan.

3 Place on MEDIUM heat and stir until sugar is dissolved.

4 Bring mixture to a boil and boil for 3 minutes. Remove from heat.

5 Add soda cracker crumbs, nuts, vanilla extract, and crunchy peanut butter and mix quickly.

6 Beat with an electric mixer until mixture is thick enough to drop from a teaspoon onto the prepared pan. Allow to set at room temperature.

Coconut Peanut Butter Cups

1 cup creamy peanut butter
1/2 cup granulated sugar
1 large egg
1/2 cup sweetened condensed milk
2 cups flaked coconut
50—1-1/4 inch paper baking cups

1 Preheat oven to 325°F. Place paper baking cups on cookie sheet. Set aside.

2 Combine the peanut butter, sugar, and egg in a mixing bowl. Blend thoroughly with an electric mixer on LOW speed.

3 Press 1-1/2 teaspoons of this mixture into the bottom of each paper cup.

4 In a separate bowl, combine the sweetened condensed milk and coconut. Mix well with a wooden spoon.

5 Add one teaspoonful of the coconut mixture on top of the peanut butter mixture in each cup.

6 Bake 20 minutes, until tops are lightly browned.

7 Remove from the oven. Cool on a wire rack. Remove from the paper cups. Store in a cool place.

Tasty Nut Brittle

2 cups granulated sugar
1 tablespoon butter
1 teaspoon vanilla extract
2 cups shelled hazelnuts, coarsely chopped and lightly toasted
1 cup shredded coconut, lightly toasted

1 Lightly butter a large cookie sheet. Set aside.

2 Put the sugar in a large heavy saucepan.

3 Cook, stirring constantly, over MEDIUM heat, until sugar is melted (about 15 minutes). Stir in the butter, LOWER the heat, and cook until the mixture is amber (about 3 to 5 minutes).

4 Remove from heat and immediately stir in the vanilla extract, hazelnuts, and coconut.

5 Pour mixture onto the prepared cookie sheet and spread out using the back of a wooden spoon to a thickness of about 1/3 inch.

6 When the brittle is completely cooled, loosen from the sheet and break into pieces.

7 Store in an airtight container at room temperature for up to 1 month.

Peanut Butter Roll

2 cups powdered sugar (see p8)
2 tablespoons butter (at room temperature)
2 tablespoons whipping cream
1/2 teaspoon vanilla extract
3/4 cup smooth peanut butter

1 Put the powdered sugar, butter, whipping cream, and vanilla extract in a medium bowl and combine with your hands to the consistency of pie dough.

2 Divide dough into 2 portions.

3 Roll out each portion separately, between sheets of wax paper.

4 Spread each portion with peanut butter and roll up like a jelly roll.

5 Cut in 1/2 inch slices. Store in the refrigerator.

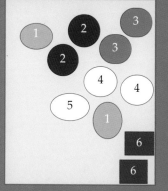

1 *Tasty Nut Brittle, p48*
2 *Microwave Peanut Butter Cups, p50*
3 *Surprise Drops, p47*
4 *Peanut Butter Roll, p49*
5 *Coconut Peanut Butter Cups, p48*
6 *Fruit Jellies, p50*

49

Microwave Peanut Butter Cups

1 cup semi-sweet chocolate chips
1-1/2 cups peanut butter
2 tablespoons butter
30 small foil candy cups

1. Combine the chocolate chips, 2/3 cup peanut butter, and butter in a large glass measuring cup.
2. Microwave on HIGH for 1-1/2 to 2 minutes, until chocolate is melted (p11). Stir until smooth.
3. Pour half of this mixture into the bottom of small candy cups.
4. Put the remaining peanut butter in a small microwave-safe bowl and microwave on HIGH for 1 minute.
5. Spoon peanut butter on top of the chocolate layer in the foil candy cups.
6. Cover with the remaining chocolate mixture. Cool. Store in a covered container.

Fruit Jellies

1 cup raspberry jam
2 cups strawberry jam
1 cup unsweetened applesauce
1-3/8 cups granulated sugar
1/8 cup lemon juice
1 cup pecans, finely chopped
1 pound chocolate-flavored candy coatings, for dipping (optional)

1. Line a cookie sheet with wax paper and lightly spray with vegetable oil.
2. Combine jams, applesauce, and sugar in a large heavy saucepan. Cook and stir over MEDIUM heat until sugar is dissolved. Wash down sides of pan frequently with a pastry brush dipped in hot water to remove sugar crystals. Add a candy thermometer.
3. Continue cooking over MEDIUM HIGH heat, stirring constantly, to 238°F (soft ball stage, p10).
4. Remove from heat.
5. Add the lemon juice and stir. Add pecans and stir.
6. Pour the finished jelly onto the prepared pan. Spread jelly to a uniform thickness. Allow to set at room temperature overnight.
7. When set, slice into 1/2 inch squares using a vegetable-oil-coated knife.
8. Put chocolate-flavored coatings in a microwave-safe bowl and microwave on DEFROST for 5 minutes, stirring 3 times. Remove from the microwave.
9. Drop each piece of fruit jelly into the melted chocolate. Evenly coat all sides. Lift jelly out using a dipping spoon.
10. Allow to set on wax paper. Store in a covered container.

Cashew Crunch

1 cup butter
2 cups brown sugar
1/3 cup water
1 cup cashews (or pecans), toasted and chopped
1/2 pound white vanilla-flavored candy coatings

1 Butter a 9 x 13 inch pan. Set aside.

2 Combine the butter, sugar, and water in a large heavy saucepan. Cook and stir over MEDIUM heat until sugar dissolves. Wash down sides of pan frequently with a pastry brush dipped in hot water to remove sugar crystals. Add a candy thermometer.

3 Continue cooking over MEDIUM heat, stirring constantly, to 300°F to 308°F (hard crack stage, p10).

4 Remove from heat and stir in the nuts. Pour into the prepared pan. Allow to cool.

5 Melt the candy coatings (p11). Spread half on the candy mixture in the pan. Allow to set.

6 Invert on wax paper and remove from the pan. Coat the other side with the remaining melted coatings. Allow to cool at room temperature.

7 When cool and firm break into pieces.

Nature's Goody Munchies

1/2 cup butter
3/4 cup brown sugar, packed
1 cup flaked coconut
1/3 cup sesame seeds
1 teaspoon cinnamon
1 cup walnuts, coarsely chopped
1/2 cup apricots, dried and chopped
1-1/2 cups instant oatmeal
1/2 cup toasted wheat germ
1/3 cup honey

1 Line a jelly roll pan with wax paper. Set aside.

2 Combine the butter and brown sugar in a 10 x 8 inch microwave-safe baking dish. Microwave on HIGH 1-1/2 minutes, or until melted.

3 Add the remaining ingredients and mix thoroughly. Spread evenly in the baking dish.

4 Microwave on HIGH 6 minutes or until bubbly, stirring every 2 minutes.

5 Scrape mixture onto the prepared pan. Spread evenly to a thickness of 1 inch. Score while still warm. Allow to cool completely.

6 When cool, cut into squares.

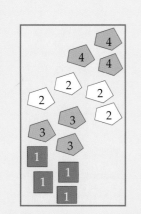

Nutty Brittle

1 cup granulated sugar
1 cup water
1 cup light corn syrup
1-1/2 cups cashews
1 teaspoon vanilla extract
1/2 teaspoon baking soda

1 Butter a cookie sheet. Set aside.

2 Combine the sugar, water, and corn syrup in a large heavy saucepan.

3 Cook over MEDIUM HIGH heat, stirring occasionally, until mixture comes to a boil. Wash down sides of pan frequently with a pastry brush dipped in hot water to remove sugar crystals. Add a candy thermometer.

4 Continue to cook on MEDIUM heat, to 275°F (soft crack stage, p10), about 20 minutes.

5 Add the cashews. Continue cooking and stirring to 305°F (hard crack stage, p10), about 5 to 7 minutes longer.

6 Remove from heat. Quickly stir in vanilla extract and baking soda.

7 Pour onto the prepared cookie sheet, pushing brittle to edges of sheet with the back of a wooden spoon.

8 As the candy cools, stretch it out thinly by lifting and pulling from the edges, using 2 forks (p14).

9 When the brittle is completely cooled, loosen from the sheet and break into pieces.

10 Store in an airtight container at room temperature for up to 1 month.

Peanut Brittle

1 cup granulated sugar
1/2 cup light corn syrup
1/8 teaspoon salt
1-1/2 cups peanuts, salted and roasted
1 tablespoon butter or margarine
1 teaspoon vanilla extract
1 teaspoon baking soda

1 Butter a jelly roll pan. Set aside.

2 Combine the sugar, corn syrup, and salt in a large microwave-safe bowl and microwave at HIGH for 5 minutes.

3 Stir in the peanuts.

4 Microwave 3 minutes longer, stirring after 2 minutes, until syrup and peanuts are lightly browned.

5 Stir in the butter, vanilla extract, and baking soda, until mixture is light and foamy.

6 Spread to a thickness of about 1/4 inch on the prepared pan. Allow to cool. Break in pieces.

Date Roll Candy

2 cups granulated sugar
4 tablespoons butter, melted
1 tablespoon light corn syrup
3/4 cup half and half cream
1 cup dates, finely chopped
3/4 cup walnuts, chopped
1/2 cup coconut
1 teaspoon vanilla extract

1 Dampen a clean tea towel and set aside on a counter.

2 Combine the sugar, butter, corn syrup, and cream or milk in a large heavy saucepan.

3 Heat to boiling over MEDIUM heat, stirring constantly. Add a candy thermometer.

4 Cook over MEDIUM heat, stirring occasionally, to 225°F. Add the dates and cook to 238°F (soft ball stage, p10), about 10 minutes. Remove from heat. Cool.

5 Add the walnuts, coconut, and vanilla extract.

6 Beat with a wooden spoon until mixture holds its shape.

7 Place on the damp tea towel and roll mixture into a long roll.

8 Allow to set until firm. Slice to serve.

54

Sugar Snowballs

1-1/2 cups dried apricots, coarsely chopped
1 cup golden raisins
1/3 cup amaretto liqueur
grated rind of 1 orange
2 cups shredded coconut
1/2 cup blanched almonds, lightly toasted
1/2 cup powdered sugar, for rolling

1 Line 2 cookie sheets with wax paper. Set aside.

2 Combine all ingredients except the powdered sugar in a food processor fitted with a steel chopping blade. Process until the mixture is finely chopped and blended.

3 Place powdered sugar in a shallow bowl for coating the balls.

4 Using a teaspoonful of the fruit mixture, roll into balls.

5 Roll into the powdered sugar and place on the prepared sheets. Allow to stand for 1 hour.

6 Place each candy in a paper candy cup or pack in a tightly covered container.

Photograph on p55, *Sugar Snowballs*

Special Molasses Popcorn Balls

1-1/4 cups granulated sugar
1-1/2 cups brown sugar
3/4 cup light corn syrup
1/4 cup molasses
1/2 cup water
2 tablespoons butter
1/2 teaspoon salt
1 teaspoon vanilla extract
16 cups popped corn

1 Line a cookie sheet with wax paper. Set aside.

2 Combine the sugars, corn syrup, molasses, and water in a large heavy saucepan.

3 Stir over MEDIUM heat until sugars are dissolved. Add a candy thermometer.

4 Cook over MEDIUM heat to 284°F (soft crack stage, p10).

5 Remove from heat and add the butter, salt, and vanilla extract.

6 Blend well and pour over the popcorn. Stir with a wooden spoon.

7 Grease your hands with a little butter and shape the mixture into popcorn balls.

8 Set on the prepared pan to harden.

Caramel Popcorn

8 cups popped corn
30 vanilla caramels
2 tablespoons water
1/8 teaspoon salt

1 Keep the popcorn hot and crisp in an oven set at 300°F.

2 Combine the caramels and water in a large glass measuring cup. Microwave on HIGH for 1 minute. Stir until melted and smooth (or melt in double boiler, p11).

3 Transfer the hot popcorn to a large buttered bowl.

4 Pour the melted caramels over the popcorn and toss until well coated.

5 Butter your hands and carefully shape the mixture into 2 inch or 6 inch balls or press popcorn into buttered molds in the shape of trees, snowmen, a Santa, even a turkey. Decorate appropriately.

upper right *Carmel Popcorn, p57*
lower left *Special Molasses Popcorn Balls, p56*

Corn Balls

24 paper muffin cups
12 ounces semi-sweet chocolate chips
2 cups plain popped corn
2 cups carmel corn
2 cups salted peanuts
candy decorations

1 Line muffin pans with paper cups. Set aside.

2 Put chocolate chips in a microwave-safe bowl and microwave 2 minutes on MEDIUM power. Stir. Remove from the microwave.

3 Stir in the plain popcorn, carmel corn, and peanuts. Stir gently with a wooden spoon until well coated.

4 Drop mixture by tablespoonfuls into paper cups. Sprinkle on candy decorations.

5 Refrigerate until set.

Molasses Popcorn Pops

1 cup light molasses
1 cup granulated sugar
1 teaspoon salt
16 cups popped corn
16—5-ounce paper drink cups (or 28—3 ounce)
16 sucker sticks
colored plastic wrap and curling ribbon (optional)

1 Butter a large bowl. Set aside.

2 Combine the molasses, sugar, and salt in a large heavy saucepan. Add a candy thermometer.

3 Cook over MEDIUM heat to 260°F (hard ball stage, p10).

4 Put the popcorn in the prepared bowl and pour on the hot syrup. Mix until well coated.

5 Press popcorn mixture in the drink cups and insert sucker sticks. Allow to cool completly.

6 Push on the bottom of the paper cups to remove the popcorn pops. To decorate for a party, wrap in colored plastic wrap and tie with colored curling ribbon.

Movie Time Karamel Jack

10 cups popped corn
2-1/4 cups brown sugar
1/2 cup light corn syrup
1/2 cup water
1/2 cup butter or margarine
2 teaspoons salt
1 tablespoon vanilla extract
1 cup mixed nuts, salted (almonds, cashews, peanuts, pecans)

1 Keep popcorn hot and crisp in an oven set at 300°F.

2 Butter a 12 x 18 inch cookie sheet and a large bowl. Set aside.

3 Combine the sugar, corn syrup, water, butter, and salt in a large heavy saucepan. Cook and stir until sugar dissolves. Add a candy thermometer.

4 Cook over MEDIUM heat, stirring occasionally, to 284°F (soft crack stage, p10).

5 Remove from heat and stir in the vanilla extract.

6 Combine nuts and popcorn in the large buttered bowl.

7 Pour syrup over the mixture and mix to completely coat the popcorn.

8 Press into bite-size clusters and set on the prepared pan.

9 Cool completely. Store in an airtight container.

Taffy Apples

9 medium apples, washed and dried, not peeled
9 wooden skewers
6 cups granulated sugar
3 cups water
3/4 teaspoon cream of tartar
1/4 teaspoon red paste food coloring

1 Line a cookie sheet with parchment paper. Set aside.

2 Stick a wooden skewer into each apple.

3 Combine the sugar, water, and cream of tartar in a large heavy saucepan. Stir until sugar crystals are dissolved. Add a candy thermometer.

4 Cook without stirring over HIGH heat to 284°F (soft crack stage, p10).

5 Remove from heat and add the paste food coloring. Place the pan in hot water to keep taffy from hardening.

6 Dip apples into the taffy mixture until bottom half of apples is completely coated. Add a few drops of water if taffy mixture thickens.

7 Place on the prepared cookie sheet to cool.

1 *Movie Time Karamel Jack, p59*
2 *Baked Caramel Corn, p60*
3 *Caramel Apples, p61*
4 *Taffy Apples, p60*
5 *Molasses Popcorn Pops, p59*

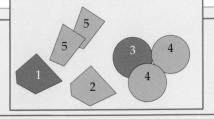

Baked Caramel Corn

1-1/2 cups popping corn or 36 cups popped corn
1 cup butter
2 cups brown sugar, packed
1/2 cup light corn syrup
1 teaspoon salt
1/2 teaspoon baking soda
1 teaspoon vanilla extract

1 Put the popped corn in a large roasting pan.

2 Put the butter in a large heavy saucepan and melt over MEDIUM heat.

3 Stir in the sugar, corn syrup, and salt.

4 Bring the mixture to a boil, stirring constantly, and boil for about 5 minutes. Remove from heat. Add baking soda and vanilla extract. Stir well.

5 Pour the hot mixture over the popcorn, mixing well.

6 Bake in a 250°F oven for 1 hour, stirring every 15 minutes. Remove from the oven and cool. Baked Caramel Corn freezes well.

Caramel Apples

6 medium apples, washed and dried, not peeled
6 wooden skewers
50 caramels
2 tablespoons water
1/8 teaspoon salt
1 cup pecans or almonds, finely chopped

1 Line a cookie sheet with wax paper. Set aside.

2 Stick a wooden skewer into each apple.

3 Melt the caramels using a double boiler (p11) with 2 tablespoons of water. Add salt and stir until smooth.

4 Dip apples in the caramel mixture until bottom half of apples is completely coated. Add a few drops of water if caramel thickens.

5 Roll coated apples in nuts.

6 Place on the prepared cookie sheet to cool.

Popcorn Christmas Tree Place Cards

1-1/3 cups popping corn or 32 cups popped corn
3 cups white sugar
1 cup light corn syrup
1 cup water
3/4 cup butter
1 teaspoon salt
2 teaspoons vinegar
2 teaspoons vanilla extract
green paste food coloring (a bit on the end of a toothpick)

1 Butter a 6-mini-tree pan. Put the popcorn in a large bowl and line a cookie sheet with wax paper. Set aside.

2 Combine the sugar, corn syrup, water, butter, salt, and vinegar in a large heavy saucepan.

3 Cook over MEDIUM heat until sugar dissolves. Add a candy thermometer.

4 Cook without stirring to 260°F (hard ball stage, p10).

5 Remove from heat and add vanilla extract and paste food coloring to the desired shade (see p13).

6 Pour the colored syrup over the popcorn and coat well.

7 Press the colored popcorn into the prepared pan. When tree shapes are set remove the trees from the pan onto the prepared cookie sheet.

8 Use as place names for Christmas dinner parties, birthday parties, or festive celebrations. Write guest names on each popcorn tree with colored gel or icing.

Christmas Lollipops

1/4 cup butter or margarine
1/2 cup light corn syrup
3/4 cup granulated sugar
4 drops of cinnamon or cherry candy oil flavoring
red paste food coloring (a bit on the end of a toothpick)
18 lollipop sticks
candy decorations

1 Butter a cookie sheet and arrange lollipop sticks on the sheet. Set aside.

2 Combine the butter, corn syrup, and sugar in a medium-size heavy saucepan.

3 Cook and stir over MEDIUM heat until sugar is dissolved. Add a candy thermometer.

4 Continue to cook to 270°F (soft crack stage, p10), stirring frequently.

5 Stir in the paste food coloring and oil flavoring.

6 Drop mixture by tablespoonfuls over the end of each lollipop stick. While lollipops are hot, press on candy decorations.

7 Cool lollipops thoroughly before removing from the cookie sheet.

NOTE Use candy oil flavoring and paste food coloring for best results (p13).

Russian Mints

2-1/4 cups chocolate chips
2 cups mini-marshmallows
1 cup butter, at room temperature
4 cups granulated sugar
10 ounces evaporated milk
1 teaspoon mint extract
3 cups chocolate-flavored candy coatings

1 Combine the chocolate chips, marshmallows, and butter in a large bowl. Set aside.

2 Butter a 9 x 13 inch square pan. Set aside.

3 Combine the sugar and evaporated milk in a large heavy saucepan. Bring to a boil on HIGH heat. Reduce heat to MEDIUM and boil 10 minutes. Stir in the mint extract.

4 Pour this mixture over the marshmallows, chocolate chips, and butter in the bowl. Stir to blend.

5 Pour into the prepared pan.

6 Place in the refrigerator overnight to set.

7 Cut in small squares with a knife. Melt chocolate coatings (p11). Using a dipping spoon, coat each square (p11) with melted candy coatings. Set on wax paper to harden.

Chocolate Butter Crunch

1 cup butter
1 cup granulated sugar
2 tablespoons water
1 tablespoon light corn syrup
3/4 cup nuts, finely chopped
6 ounces semi-sweet chocolate chips

1 Butter a 10 x 15 inch jelly roll pan. Set aside.

2 Melt the butter in a large heavy saucepan over LOW heat.

3 Add the sugar, water, and corn syrup. Heat to boiling over MEDIUM heat, stirring constantly. Wash down sides of pan frequently with a pastry brush dipped in hot water to remove sugar crystals. Add a candy thermometer.

4 Cook over MEDIUM heat, stirring constantly, to 284°F (soft crack stage, p10). Remove from heat.

5 Stir in the nuts. Pour candy mixture onto the prepared pan. Spread to 1/4 inch thickness. Cool.

6 Melt chocolate chips (p11). Spread half the chocolate over the crunch. Allow to set.

7 When firm, turn crunch over and spread with the remaining chocolate. Allow to set.

8 Break into pieces. Store in an airtight container in a cool place.

Chocolate Turtles

144 small pecan halves
36 light caramels
1 cup chocolate-flavored candy coatings

1. Butter 2 cookie sheets.

2. Arrange pecan halves in groups of 4 (for each turtle) on both prepared pans.

3. Unwrap caramels and center one caramel atop each cluster of nuts.

4. Bake in a 325°F oven for 8 to 10 minutes (until caramels soften).

5. Remove from the oven and flatten each caramel with a buttered spatula.

6. Place pans on a wire rack and cool slightly.

7. Melt the candy coatings in the microwave (p11) and add the melted coatings on top of each turtle with the spatula or a spoon. Allow to harden.

Almond Raisin Bark

1 cup almonds, skins on
1 pound white chocolate-flavored candy coatings
1 cup raisins

1. Line a cookie sheet with wax paper. Set aside.

2. Place the almonds on another cookie sheet and heat in a 350°F oven for 10 minutes, stirring twice.

3. Put candy coatings in a large measuring cup and microwave on DEFROST for 5 minutes, stirring 3 times. Remove from the microwave.

4. Stir in the raisins and toasted almonds.

5. Pour onto the prepared cookie sheet.

6. Allow to cool, then break into pieces.

NOTE Raisins may be omitted for an almond-only flavor.

Peanut Butter Cherry Chocolate Balls

3 tablespoons butter
3/4 cup peanut butter
1-3/4 cups powdered sugar (see p8)
1 jar maraschino cherries with stems
2 cups chocolate-flavored candy coatings

1 Line a cookie sheet with wax paper. Set aside.

2 In a medium bowl, cream the butter. Then add the peanut butter and powdered sugar. Mix well. (Mixture may seem dry but, when worked with your hands, the mixture will soften.)

3 Drain the maraschino cherries and set on paper towels.

4 Form a ball of peanut butter mixture around each cherry. Place on the prepared sheet. Chill in the refrigerator for 1/2 hour.

5 Melt the candy coatings (p11).

6 Remove cherry balls from the refrigerator and dip (p11) in the melted candy coatings.

7 Peanut Butter Cherry Chocolate Balls freeze well. Remove from the freezer just before serving. Place candies in foil or colored paper candy cups.

Marzipan

5 tablespoons glucose
2 cups almond paste
2 cups powdered sugar (see p8)
red, green, orange, yellow paste food colorings
oil food flavorings
whole cloves and cocoa powder for decorations (optional)
1/2 cup light corn syrup
1 tablespoon water

1 Put glucose in a microwave-safe bowl. Microwave on HIGH for 20 seconds.

2 Stir the warmed glucose into the almond paste.

3 Add powdered sugar and blend. Knead the mixture until the marzipan has a consistency of pie dough.

4 Divide marzipan into 5 portions. Do not color one of the portions.

5 Dip individual toothpicks into red, green, orange, and yellow paste colorings. Add a separate color to each portion of marzipan and knead marzipan until color is evenly mixed. While kneading in the color, add a few drops of oil flavoring (see colors and flavors, p13).

6 Sprinkle powdered sugar on the counter and roll each marzipan section with your hand into a long rope, 1 inch thick.

7 Slice the rope into pieces the sizes of the fruits or vegetables you desire.

8 Shape and roll these pieces into balls or tapered shapes. Make apples, pears, bananas, carrots. Shape potatoes from uncolored portions of marzipan. Use a wooden skewer to make eyes in the potatoes. Use a sharp knife to make grooves in carrots and a toothpick or wooden skewer to make holes. Add cloves for stems. Roll potatoes in cocoa powder. Roll out green marzipan with rolling pin and cut shaped leaves and strands for fruits and vegetables.

9 Thin the corn syrup with 1 tablespoon water. Heat slightly in the microwave on HIGH for 5 seconds. Brush on marzipan fruits and vegetables as a glaze.

Coconut Chocolate Bars

3/4 pound coconut
1/4 pound chopped candied cherries
1/4 pound whole light raisins
1/4 cup pecans, chopped
1-1/2 cups light corn syrup
1 cup granulated sugar
1/2 cup water
1 pound dark chocolate-flavored candy coatings

1 Butter a 9 x 13-inch square pan. Set aside.

2 Combine the coconut, candied cherries, raisins, and pecans in a large bowl. Set aside.

3 Combine the corn syrup, sugar, and water in a large heavy saucepan. Stir over HIGH heat until sugar is dissolved. STOP STIRRING. Add a candy thermometer.

4 Continue cooking over MEDIUM heat to 238°F (soft ball stage, p10).

5 Remove from heat and pour over the dry ingredients in bowl. Mix well.

6 Press evenly in the prepared pan. Allow to cool completely, then cut into bars.

7 Dip bars (p11) in melted candy coatings (p11).

8 Place bars on wax paper to set. Bars may be wrapped in colored foil or clear plastic wrap.

Rum Raisin Clusters

2 cups raisins
1/2 cup rum
1 pound chocolate-flavored candy coatings

1 Put raisins and rum in a jar for a few days until raisins have absorbed most of the rum. Drain well.

2 Put chocolate-flavored candy coatings in a microwave-safe bowl and microwave on DEFROST for 5 minutes, stirring 3 times. Add the raisins.

3 Quickly drop by teaspoonfuls onto wax paper. (If mixture thickens return to the microwave and remelt in 30-second intervals.)

4 Allow to cool.

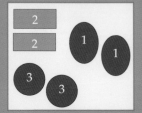

top photo
1 *Easter Egg Chocolates, p72*
2 *Coconut Chocolate Bars, p70*
3 *Rum Raisin Clusters, p70*

bottom photo
Orange Cheese Balls, p72

Easter Egg Chocolates

1/2 cup light corn syrup
12 large marshmallows
1-3/4 cups coconut
1 teaspoon vanilla extract
1/4 teaspoon almond extract
1 pound chocolate-flavored candy coatings, for dipping

1 Line a 15 x 10 inch jelly roll pan with wax paper. Set aside.

2 Combine the corn syrup and marshmallows in a large heavy saucepan.

3 Cook and stir over MEDIUM heat until marshmallows are melted. Remove from heat.

4 Using a wooden spoon, stir in the coconut and vanilla and almond extracts. Refrigerate 10 minutes until mixture is cool enough to handle.

5 Butter your hands and shape mixture into small egg shapes. Place on the prepared pan. Let stand 1/2 hour before dipping.

6 When cool, use a dipping spoon and coat each egg (p11) with melted candy coatings (p11).

NOTE Marshmallows can be melted in a microwave before combining with corn syrup using MEDIUM power for 1 minute.

Orange Cheese Balls

2 pounds vanilla-flavored candy coatings
8 ounces cream cheese (at room temperature)
1 cup orange marmalade
3 tablespoons grated orange peel
1/4 teaspoon pineapple extract
1/4 teaspoon each lemon and orange oil food flavorings
3 cups instant dry milk
3 cups powdered sugar (see p8)
3 cups toasted fine coconut (optional)

1 Line a cookie sheet with wax paper. Set aside.

2 Melt the candy coatings (p11).

3 Using an electric mixer on MEDIUM speed, beat the cream cheese and marmalade together in a mixing bowl.

4 Reduce speed to LOW and add orange peel, pineapple extract, and lemon and orange flavorings.

5 Blend in the dry milk and sifted powdered sugar. Beat on HIGH speed with an electric mixer for 2 minutes.

6 Put mixer on MEDIUM speed and add melted coatings. Allow to cool.

7 When cool, roll into balls and then in toasted fine coconut. Set on the prepared pan.

NOTE Balls may also be dipped in melted orange coatings (p11).

Easy Chocolate-Dipped Party Favorites

A variety of snack foods may be dipped in melted coatings.
Place in bowls for favorite party munchies.

2 cups chocolate-flavored candy coatings
2 cups vanilla-flavored candy coatings
large salted pretzels, saltine crackers, broken candy cane pieces,
raisins, salted nuts, dry chow mein noodles, jelly beans,
large marshmallows

1 Put each coating in separate microwave-safe bowls and microwave on DEFROST for 5 minutes. Stir 2 or 3 times. If flavored coatings become thick while dipping the party munchies, reheat in the microwave, as needed.

2 Dip half of a large salted pretzel in vanilla- or chocolate-flavored candy coatings. Place on wax paper to set.

3 Dip crackers in vanilla- or chocolate-flavored candy coatings. Remove with a dipping spoon and top with colorful sprinkles. Allow to set on wax paper.

4 Dip pieces of broken candy canes into chocolate-flavored candy coatings. Remove with a dipping spoon. Allow to set on wax paper.

5 Stir raisins or salted nuts into vanilla- or milk-chocolate-flavored candy coatings. Place in clusters on wax paper. Allow to set.

6 Stir dry chow mein noodles into vanilla- or milk-chocolate-flavored candy coatings. Drop by teaspoonfuls onto parchment paper. Allow to set.

7 Stir 1/2 cup jelly beans into 2 cups chocolate-flavored candy coatings. Spread out on wax paper. When set, break into pieces.

8 Place 2 or 3 marshmallows on a sucker stick. Dip in chocolate-flavored candy coatings and roll in toasted coconut or chopped nuts.

1 *Potato Candy, p75*
2 *Tiger Butter, p75*

Potato Candy

1 medium-size potato
1 teaspoon vanilla extract
6-1/2 cups powdered sugar, sifted (see p8)
6 tablespoons peanut butter

1 Peel, cook, drain, and mash the potato with a fork. Blend in vanilla extract.

2 Stir in powdered sugar until mixture is thick and rolls easily. Divide into 2 portions.

3 Sprinkle counter with powdered sugar. Roll portions into 8 inch squares on the counter.

4 Spread peanut butter over each square and roll like a jelly roll.

5 Wrap each roll in wax paper and cool in the refrigerator for at least 3 hours.

6 Cut into 1/2 inch slices. Store in the refrigerator in an airtight container.

Tiger Butter

1 cup chocolate-flavored candy coatings
1 cup vanilla-flavored candy coatings
1/2 cup smooth peanut butter

1 Line a 9-inch square pan with wax paper. Set aside.

2 Melt (p11) chocolate-flavored candy coatings. Put in a medium bowl. Set aside.

3 Melt vanilla-flavored candy coatings. Put in another bowl and add the peanut butter. Mix well.

4 Add melted chocolate-flavored candy coatings to peanut butter mixture, stirring slightly.

5 Pour into the prepared pan. Using a table knife, stir swirls of the light and dark mixtures to give a marbled look.

6 Allow to set at room temperature until solid. Cut into 1 inch squares.

Caramel-Coated Marshmallows

60 wrapped caramels
2 tablespoons water
36 large marshmallows
36 paper candy cups

1 Put caramels and water in a large glass measuring cup. Place in the microwave on DEFROST for 2 minutes or until melted. Remove from the microwave and stir until smooth and well blended.

2 Using a dipping spoon, dip (p11) each marshmallow in caramel.

3 Place on wax paper to set. When set, place in paper candy cups and serve.

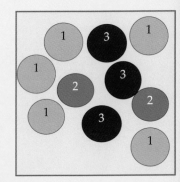

1 *Caramel-Coated Marshmallows, p76*
2 *Pralines, p76*
3 *Chocolate Peanut Butter Cups, p77*

Pralines

6 ounce package of vanilla pudding
1-1/2 cups brown sugar, firmly packed
1/2 cup evaporated milk
1 teaspoon butter
2 cups pecan halves

1 Combine the pudding mix, sugar, evaporated milk, and butter in a large heavy saucepan.

2 Heat slowly on MEDIUM heat and stir until sugar dissolves. Wash down sides of pan with a pastry brush dipped in hot water to remove sugar crystals. Add a candy thermometer.

3 Cook without stirring to 238°F (soft ball stage, p10).

4 Remove from heat. Stir in the pecans.

5 Beat with a wooden spoon 2 to 3 minutes, until mixture starts to thicken.

6 Quickly drop by tablespoonfuls, 2 inches apart on wax paper. (If mixture hardens as you work, set the pan over hot water.)

7 Allow to set. Store in a covered container.

Chocolate Peanut Butter Cups

10 ounces milk-chocolate-flavored candy coatings
1-1/2 cups chunky peanut butter
30 small foil cups

1 Melt (p11) the candy coatings.

2 Add the chunky peanut butter and mix thoroughly.

3 Spoon into small foil cups. Place in the refrigerator to set.

Rocky Road Candy

12 ounces semi-sweet chocolate chips
12 ounces butterscotch chips
1/2 cup butter
10 ounces mini-marshmallows
1 cup nuts

1 Butter a 9 x 13 inch pan. Set aside.

2 Combine the semi-sweet chocolate chips, butterscotch chips, and butter in a large microwave-safe mixing bowl.

3 Microwave at DEFROST for 5 minutes, until melted. Stir. Remove from the microwave.

4 Stir in the marshmallows and nuts.

5 Spread in the prepared pan.

6 Refrigerate 2 hours, until set. Cut into squares.

Chocolate Crunch Clusters

1 cup chocolate-flavored candy coatings
1/2 cup peanuts, coarsely chopped
2/3 cup sugar-coated puffed wheat
1/2 cup mini-marshmallows

1 Melt the candy coatings (p11). Put in a large bowl.

2 Add the remaining ingredients and mix well.

3 Drop mixture by teaspoonfuls on wax paper.

4 Allow to set.

Peanut Butter Heavenly Hash

1 pound milk-chocolate-flavored candy coatings
1 cup chunky peanut butter
1 cup mini-marshmallows

1 Line an 8-inch square pan with foil. Set aside.

2 Melt the candy coatings (p11).

3 Put coatings in a large bowl and stir in the chunky peanut butter.

4 Cool slightly and add the marshmallows.

5 Pour into the prepared pan and allow to harden.

6 Cut into squares with a knife.

Chocolate Raisin Nut Clusters

6 ounces semi-sweet chocolate chips
1 cup salted peanuts
1 cup raisins

1 Line a cookie sheet with wax paper. Set aside.

2 Combine the chocolate chips, peanuts, and raisins in a large microwave-safe casserole dish and cover.

3 Microwave at DEFROST for 4 to 5 minutes, until chocolate is melted.

4 Stir mixture and drop by teaspoonfuls onto wax paper.

5 Chill in the refrigerator until firm.

1 *Rocky Road Candy, p78*
2 *Chocolate Crunch Clusters, p78*
3 *Peanut Butter Heavenly Hash, p78*
4 *Chocolate Raisin Nut Clusters, p79*

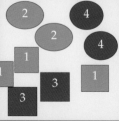

Easy Toffee

1-1/2 cups brown sugar
1/2 cup water
1/4 cup vinegar
2 tablespoons butter
1/4 cup raisins or chopped nuts (optional)

1 Butter an 8-inch square pan. Set aside.

2 Combine the sugar, water, and vinegar in a medium-size heavy saucepan and stir over MEDIUM heat until sugar dissolves. Wash down sides of pan frequently with a pastry brush dipped in hot water to remove sugar crystals. Add a candy thermometer.

3 Bring the mixture to a boil and cook without stirring to 258°F (hard ball stage, p10).

4 Remove from heat. Add butter, stir, and pour into the prepared pan. Add raisins or nuts, if desired.

5 Allow to set. Cut into squares with a knife.

1 *Easy Toffee, p80*
2 *Peanut Butter Candy, p80*
3 *Raisin Clusters, p82*
4 *Coconut Bon Bons, p82*

Peanut Butter Candy

BOTTOM LAYER
1-1/2 cups peanut butter
1-3/4 cups brown sugar
1-3/4 cups powdered sugar (see p8)
1/4 cup butter, melted

TOP LAYER
1 cup semi-sweet chocolate chips
1/4 cup butter

1 Butter a 9 x 13 inch pan. Set aside.

2 Combine all bottom layer ingredients in a large bowl. Mix well.

3 Press into the prepared pan.

4 Combine chocolate chips and butter for the top layer in a large glass measuring cup.

5 Microwave at HIGH for 2 minutes. Stir until creamy.

6 Spread over the peanut butter mixture. Score into squares with a knife

7 Cool completely. Cut into squares.

Coconut Bon Bons

3/4 cup white or clear corn syrup
2-1/2 cups fine coconut, lightly toasted
2-1/4 cups colored candy coatings

1 Put the corn syrup in a large glass measuring cup and heat in a microwave on HIGH for 1 minute.

2 Remove from the microwave and add the lightly toasted coconut. Mix well. Let stand about 1/2 hour to cool.

3 With clean wet hands, roll mixture into 3/4 inch balls.

4 Melt the candy coatings (p11)—3/4 cup each of pink, yellow, and green.

5 Using a dipping spoon, dip (p11) balls into pink, yellow, or green candy coatings, and place on wax paper to harden.

NOTE Candy coatings come in a variety of colors for decorating and have a vanilla flavor. Choose a color for any festive occasion and add a suitable oil food flavoring (p13).

Raisin Clusters

1/2 cup white or clear corn syrup
2 cups raisins
10 ounces chocolate-flavored candy coatings

1 Put corn syrup in a large glass measuring cup and heat in the microwave on HIGH for 1 minute.

2 Remove from the microwave. Place raisins in a large bowl and pour the heated syrup over the raisins.

3 Allow to cool then press into 1 inch balls. Allow to set 1 hour before dipping.

4 Melt the candy coatings (p11).

5 Using a dipping spoon, dip (p11) each ball into melted (p11) candy coatings. Set on wax paper to harden.

Creamy Uncooked Pecan Roll

2 cups marshmallow creme
3-1/2 cups powdered sugar (see p8)
1 teaspoon vanilla extract
1/4 teaspoon butter flavoring
1 package (14 ounces) caramels
2 teaspoons whipping cream
1/2 cup pecans, chopped

1 Combine the marshmallow creme, powdered sugar, vanilla extract, and butter flavoring in a large bowl.

2 Knead with your hands until sugar is thoroughly blended.

3 Shape into 8 rolls. Wrap each roll in plastic wrap and place in a freezer until firm (about 1 hour).

4 Melt the caramels in a large heavy saucepan over MEDIUM heat, stirring constantly. Remove from heat and add the whipping cream.

5 Dip the frozen rolls of candy into the melted caramels. Roll in chopped pecans. Allow to cool and set.

6 Wrap in plastic and store in a cool, dry place. Slice to serve.

Candy Cereal Snacks

1 pound vanilla-flavored candy coatings
2 cups Rice Chex cereal
2 cups Corn Chex cereal
2 cups Cheerios cereal
2 cups pretzels
1 cup peanuts, salted

1 Line a jelly roll pan with wax paper. Set aside.

2 Melt the candy coatings (p11). Set aside.

3 Mix the remaining ingredients together in a large bowl.

4 Pour the melted coatings over the mixture and stir until well coated.

5 Pour onto the prepared pan. Allow to set.

6 Break into bite-size pieces.

top right   *Caramel Sticks, p84*
bottom left   *Candy Cereal Snacks, p84*

Caramel Sticks

60 wrapped caramels
2 cups puffed rice
2 pounds chocolate-flavored candy coatings

1 Line a 9-inch square pan with wax paper. Set aside.

2 Unwrap caramels and put in a large heavy saucepan. Stir constantly over MEDIUM heat until melted.

3 Remove from heat. Add the puffed rice and mix well. Pour into the prepared pan. Allow candy to set until firm.

4 Remove entire candy block from the pan and slice into 3 x 1/2 inch sticks.

5 Melt the candy coatings (p11).

6 Drop the sticks of caramel candy into the melted candy coatings and coat evenly. Remove with a dipping spoon. Tap spoon on edge of pan to release excess coating.

7 Place the sticks on wax paper. Allow to set.

8 Store in an airtight container.

Chocolate-Dipped Fruit

A variety of fruits may be dipped in melted coatings.
Strawberries are the most popular. Grapes are another favorite.
Trays of dipped strawberries are great for
summer garden parties, buffets, and showers.

2 cups vanilla-flavored candy coatings
2 cups semi-sweet-chocolate-flavored candy coatings

1. Prepare fresh fruit (grapes, pineapple chunks, strawberries with stems, dried apricots, and kiwi slices). Washed fruit must be thoroughly dried.

2. Put the candy coatings in separate microwave-safe bowls and microwave on DEFROST for 5 minutes. Stir 2 or 3 times.

3. Dip the piece of fruit in the semi-sweet-chocolate-flavored candy coatings first, covering half the fruit.

4. Place on wax paper to set.

5. Dip some of the chocolate-flavored-dipped fruit pieces into the vanilla-flavored candy coatings leaving about 1/4 inch rim of dark candy coatings showing. Place on wax paper to set.

6. Arrange on a serving plate. Store in the refrigerator.

Fancy Coconut Delights

1 cup butter or margarine
1 cup milk
1 cup granulated sugar
1 cup fine coconut
2 cups graham wafer crumbs
4 cups oatmeal
2 cups vanilla-flavored candy coatings, for dipping

1 Butter a 9 x 13 inch pan. Set aside.

2 Combine the butter, milk, and sugar in a large heavy saucepan.

3 Cook and stir over MEDIUM heat until melted and mixture comes to a boil.

4 Remove from heat. Add the coconut, graham wafer crumbs, and oatmeal, and stir well.

5 Press into the prepared pan. Cover with wax paper and allow to set overnight.

6 Next day cut into fancy shapes with mini fancy cookie cutters.

7 Dip (p11) each shape in melted (p11) vanilla-flavored candy coatings. Place on wax paper.

8 Before the coatings harden decorate with chocolate or colored sprinkles.

Fancy Coconut Delights, p88

Rock & Roll Fudge Slice

12 ounces butterscotch chips
2/3 cup sweetened condensed milk
1 tablespoon water
1 tablespoon vanilla extract
1 cup raisins or mini-marshmallows

1 Butter an 8-inch square pan. Set aside.

2 Melt the butterscotch chips (p11).

3 Add the remaining ingredients and stir until smooth and shiny. Do not beat.

4 Spread in the prepared pan. Allow to set.

5 Cut into squares with a knife.

Cream Cheese Mints

1 cup granulated sugar
3 ounces cream cheese, at room temperature
1 teaspoon mint extract
green paste food coloring
3 cups powdered sugar (see p8)

1 Line a cookie sheet with wax paper. Set aside.

2 Pour the granulated sugar into a small bowl and set aside.

3 In another small bowl, combine the cream cheese, flavoring, and paste food coloring (see p13).

4 Gradually add the powdered sugar and continue to stir, until well blended.

5 As mixture thickens, start to knead mixture with your hands. Form into 1 inch balls and roll in the granulated sugar.

6 Place on the prepared cookie sheet and flatten with a fork.

7 Refrigerate until ready to serve. Store in the refrigerator.

5-Minute Fudge

2/3 cup evaporated milk
1-2/3 cups granulated sugar
1/2 teaspoon salt
1-1/2 cups mini-marshmallows
1-1/2 cups semi-sweet chocolate chips
1 teaspoon vanilla extract
1/2 cup nuts, chopped

1 Butter a 9-inch square pan. Set aside.

2 Combine the evaporated milk, sugar, and salt in a large heavy saucepan.

3 Cook over MEDIUM heat, stirring constantly. Bring mixture to a boil. Wash down sides of pan with a pastry brush dipped in hot water to remove sugar crystals. Boil 5 minutes, stirring constantly.

4 Remove from heat. Add the marshmallows, chocolate chips, vanilla extract, and nuts. Stir until marshmallows melt.

5 Pour into the prepared pan.

6 Allow to cool. Cut into squares.

Chocolate Fudge

6 ounces semi-sweet chocolate chips
1/2 cup sweetened condensed milk
1 cup powdered sugar, sifted (see p8)
1/2 teaspoon vanilla extract
1/8 teaspoon salt
1/3 cup walnuts, chopped

1 Line an 8-1/2 x 4-1/2 x 2-1/2 inch loaf pan with wax paper. Set aside.

2 Combine the chocolate chips and sweetened condensed milk in a large microwave-safe bowl.

3 Cover the bowl and microwave at MEDIUM until chocolate melts (about 1 minute), stirring once.

4 Stir in the sugar, vanilla extract, and salt. Fold in the walnuts.

5 Press into the prepared pan. Allow to stand until set. Cut into pieces with a knife.

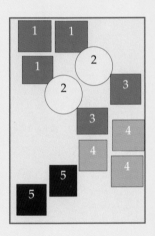

1 *Dallas Chocolate Fudge, p90*
2 *Cream Cheese Mints, p89*
3 *5-Minute Fudge, p89*
4 *Rock & Roll Fudge Slice, p88*
5 *Chocolate Fudge, p90*

Dallas Chocolate Fudge

1/4 cup milk
1/4 cup butter
6-ounce package of cooked-type chocolate pudding powder
3 cups powdered sugar, sifted (see p8)

1 Butter an 8-inch square pan. Set aside.

2 Combine the milk and butter in a large heavy saucepan.

3 Cook and stir over MEDIUM heat until mixture is melted and comes to a boil.

4 Add the chocolate pudding powder and bring to a boil again.

5 Remove from heat and stir in the sifted powdered sugar.

6 Pour into the prepared pan. Allow to cool. Cut into squares with a knife.

Golden Graham Bark

4 cups golden graham cereal
1 cup peanuts, dry roasted
2 cups vanilla-flavored candy coatings

1 Line a cookie sheet with wax paper. Set aside.

2 Put the cereal and peanuts in a large bowl.

3 Melt the candy coatings (p11) and pour over the cereal and peanuts.

4 Spread mixture on the prepared cookie sheet. Allow to set.

5 Break into serving pieces. Store in an airtight container.

right *Golden Graham Bark, p92*
left *White Chocolate Clusters, p92*

White Chocolate Clusters

1-1/2 pounds vanilla-flavored candy coatings
1 cup coconut
2 cups granola cereal with raisins and dates
1 cup nuts, chopped

1 Melt the candy coatings (p11). Put in a large bowl.

2 Add the remaining ingredients and stir.

3 Drop mixture by teaspoonfuls on wax paper.

4 Allow to set at room temperature.

5 Store in a covered container (not in the refrigerator).

Metric Conversion Chart

USA MEASURE	STANDARD METRIC MEASURE
SPOONS	
1/4 teaspoon	1 milliliter (ml)
1/2 teaspoon	2 ml
1 teaspoon	5 ml
2 teaspoons	10 ml
1 tablespoon	15 ml
2 tablespoons	25 ml
CUPS	
1/4 cup (4 tablespoons)	50 ml
1/3 cup (5-1/3 tablespoons)	75 ml
1/2 cup (8 tablespoons)	125 ml
2/3 cup (10-2/3 tablespoons)	150 ml
3/4 cup (12 tablespoons)	175 ml
1 cup (16 tablespoons)	250 ml
1-1/2 cups	375 ml
2 cups	500 ml
WEIGHTS	
10 fluid ounces	284 ml
14 fluid ounces	400 ml
1 ounce	30 grams (g)
4 ounces (1/4 pound)	125 g
8 ounces (1/2 pound)	250 g
16 ounces (1 pound)	500 g
TEMPERATURES	
65° to 70° farenheit (F)	18° to 21° centigrade (C)
110°F (lukewarm)	46°C
212°F (boiling)	100°C
250°F	120°C
SOFT BALL STAGE	
234°F to 240°F	110°C to 115°C
FIRM BALL STAGE	
244°F to 248°F	117°C to 120°C
HARD BALL STAGE	
250°F to 260°F	121°C to 128°C
SOFT CRACK STAGE	
270°F to 284°F	130°C to 140°C
HARD CRACK STAGE	
300°F to 308°F	148°C to 154°C

Index